MODERN
ANALYTICAL
AUDITING

MODERN ANALYTICAL AUDITING

Practical Guidance for Auditors and Accountants

Thomas E. McKee

Quorum Books
New York · Westport, Connecticut · London

Library of Congress Cataloging-in-Publication Data

McKee, Thomas E.
  Modern analytical auditing.

  Bibliography: p.
  Includes index.
  1. Auditing, Analytical review. I. Title.
  HF5667.M35   1989   657'.45   88-23965
  ISBN 0-89930-354-4 (lib. bdg. : alk. paper)

British Library Cataloguing in Publication Data is available.

Library of Congress Catalog Card Number: 88-23965
ISBN: 0-89930-354-4

First published in 1989 by Quorum Books

Greenwood Press, Inc.
88 Post Road West, Westport, Connecticut 06881

Printed in the United States of America

The paper used in this book complies with the
Permanent Paper Standard issued by the National
Information Standards Organization (Z39.48-1984).

10 9 8 7 6 5 4 3 2 1

Copyright Acknowledgments

The author and publisher wish to thank John Wiley & Sons, Inc., for permission to
reprint from *Corporate Financial Distress—A Complete Guide to Predicting,
Avoiding, and Dealing with Bankruptcy* by Edward I. Altman, Copyright © 1983 by
John Wiley & Sons, p. 121; figure 4.1, Current Period to Prior Period Change
Method Working Paper, reprinted with permission from *Analytical Procedures:
Improving Your Audit/Review Efficiency,* Copyright © 1988 by American Institute
of Certified Public Accountants, Inc.

To my wife Carolyn Sue, with love
To my children
Misty Dawn, Jennifer Suzanne, and Brandon Rorke
A father's heart never went so far

Contents

Figures and Tables

Figures

Tables

Preface

Analytical auditing is widely used in audit practice. It may be defined as evidence derived from an analysis of relationships among financial and nonfinancial data. Common synonyms for analytical auditing in the professional literature are "reasonableness test," "analytical review," "analytical procedures," "business approach to auditing," "performance indicator review," "audit by comparison," "audit by exception," and, most graphically, "the smell test."

Analytical auditing offers the following advantages as compared to some more traditional types of audit tests:

- Time savings by providing equivalent or stronger audit evidence, in less time.
- More objective approach to evidence generation.
- Better understanding of key factors and relationships in the client's business.
- Similar conclusions in similar circumstances.
- Better documentation of decision process.
- Productivity increases through microcomputer automation.
- A more enjoyable way to audit. An auditor can employ creativity in designing procedures rather than merely reperforming the original accounting process.

To obtain all these benefits, an audit firm must provide appropriate auditor training and underwrite initial implementation expenses.

Despite its many advantages and the widespread rapidly increasing use of analytical auditing, many auditors believe the auditing profession has not yet realized the full potential of analytical auditing. Growth and development have been limited due to a number of factors. Problems include lack of understanding about the reasoning process surrounding analytical auditing, difficulty in integrating analytical auditing with evidence theory, and lack of knowledge about the full range of potential analytical auditing techniques and their appropriate application. The widespread proliferation of microcomputers in audit practice has increased the importance of analytical auditing by dramatically increasing the number of practical analytical auditing techniques.

This book has been written to assist practicing auditors and accountants who want to obtain the benefits of analytical auditing. It provides information that can help auditors overcome the previously discussed problems. Auditors at all experience levels will benefit from this book by improving their understanding of both the underlying theory and the solutions to practical problems in applying analytical auditing. This increased understanding will provide a basis for using analytical procedures more efficiently and effectively in today's highly competitive environment.

1

The Trend Toward Increased Use of Analytical Auditing

Analytical auditing has dramatically increased in usage over the past several decades. The increased use has been greatest for financial audits. Applications in other types of audits have also grown. Analytical auditing has evolved from a nonmandatory, relatively minor part of some financial audits to a mandatory, very significant part of most financial audits. Financial auditing standards have also made it a mandatory technique on review engagements during this period. Concurrent with the increase in usage has been the expansion of analytical auditing tools from a few, mainly judgmental, techniques to a wide range of techniques that include highly objective mathematical models.

This chapter first defines the term "analytical auditing" and related basic concepts. It then explains related evidence theory and the nature of analytical auditing tests. It concludes by discussing factors which have caused the increasing use of analytical auditing and why changes in audit technology will continue this trend.

BASIC CONCEPTS

The term "analytical auditing" is defined in this book to mean evidence derived from an analysis of relationships among financial and nonfinancial data. Common synonyms in the professional literature include the terms "analytical review" and "analytical procedures." It is also sometimes called "the business approach to auditing" or "performance indicator review" (Westwick 1981: 1). Alternatively, it may be called "audit by comparison" or "audit by exception" (Casler and Crockett 1982: 42). "Analytical auditing" is used in this book because we believe that the concept is broader and frequently encompasses more than is implied by any of the previous terms. In some cases, analytical auditing may constitute the only evidence supporting a particular auditee's assertion.

An assertion is a positive statement, either express or implied, made by an auditee (entity being audited). For example, one common assertion in financial audits is "valuation," that assets are valued according to generally accepted accounting principles. Auditors confront assertions in financial, operational, and compliance audits and seek to gather evidence to prove or disprove them. However, we will limit our discussion to assertions that would be appropriate during a financial audit in order to facilitate ease of understanding for the largest number of readers. We discuss assertions in more detail in the next chapter.

The term "audit" is used for ease of expression throughout this book. It is intended to encompass not only traditional financial, compliance, and operational audits but also all other types of attestation engagements. "An attest engagement is one in which a practitioner is engaged to issue or does issue a written communication that expresses a conclusion about the reliability of a written assertion that is the responsibility of another party" (American Institute of Certified Public Accountants: 1511). This may involve assurances about financial, compliance, operational, or other assertions.

Analytical auditing techniques range from relatively simple ones, such as ratio analysis, to mathematically complex ones, such as regression analysis. The common thread binding the diverse techniques is that all are indirect tests deriving their evidential value from modeling a relationship. By "indirect tests" we mean that they do not involve determining the validity of a financial assertion by directly examining the underlying data in the accounting system supporting the assertion. Traditional techniques that test the underlying data such as vouching, confirmation, inspection, or physical examination would be categorized as "direct tests." The direct type of testing is frequently called "tests of details of transactions and balances." Analytical auditing provides evidence about a financial assertion by modeling a relationship and inferring, through an inductive reasoning process, that the modeled relationship either does or does not support the financial assertion. This is categorized as an indirect test since the support for the assertion comes from the modeling process (indirect support) as opposed to an examination of the detailed data processed by the accounting system to generate the financial amount about which the assertion is made (direct support).

USES OF ANALYTICAL AUDITING

Analytical auditing may be appropriate whenever it is desirable to model a financial relationship to generate audit evidence. Four common applications are: audit or attestation planning, tests of financial statement assertions, administrative review of audit engagement, and financial analysis. The first three applications relate primarily to uses in financial audits or similar attestation engagements. The last application encompasses nonfinancial audit uses such as use by individuals who are not professional auditors but must evaluate financial information for some purpose.

Audit or Attestation Planning

Audit or attestation planning constitutes a common use of analytical auditing. The auditor uses analytical auditing as an attention directing device to identify either unusual situations or areas of increased audit risk. Identifying these unusual situations or areas of increased audit risk before commencing audit or attestation testing allows the auditor to plan procedures to appropriately handle the unusual situation or control the increased risk. Since much audit planning takes place before the fiscal period is over, this application usually involves utilization of preliminary or interim data. For example, the auditor may calculate the ratio Number of Days Sales in Inventory to determine if there are any abnormal obsolescence risks associated with the client's inventory.

Appropriate use of analytical auditing in the planning stage of an audit allows the auditor to take a "rifle" approach as opposed to a "shotgun" approach to auditing. This means that the auditor may be able to accomplish the audit objectives by using fewer audit resources.

Tests of Financial Statement Assertions

Tests of financial statement assertions are another use of analytical auditing. The auditors' purpose in this case is to provide evidential support for a financial statement assertion. This type of use may take place in an audit, review, special report, or other attestation engagement. This application usually takes place at the end of the fiscal period since that is when the final balances for the accounts are known. Of course, it is possible to perform this type of test on interim data and appropriately update the test at year-end. An example of this type of testing would be when the auditor plots the current year amount on a carry-forward schedule and judgmentally determines if the current year amount appears reasonable based on the trend indicated on the carry-forward schedule.

Another related use is as a roll-forward test procedure to verify the reasonableness of changes in an account from an interim test date. For example, if inventory were physically observed at an interim date an auditor might use an analytical procedure to appropriately verify some or all of the changes in the inventory account that occurred between the interim testing date and fiscal year-end.

Administrative Review of Audit Engagement

Analytical auditing can also be used by a partner-in-charge or review partner to evaluate the audit scope adequacy. In this type of application the individual reviews the completed audit evidence files to determine whether an appropriate audit has been made. In doing such a review the individual may perform, formally or informally, many analytical auditing procedures to form a conclusion. For example, a reviewer may calculate selected ratios to determine if the final figures appear reasonable and those ratios may not necessarily have been calculated as part of the audit or attestation procedures. Such a review is typically done on the year-end financial data after all proposed audit adjustments have been posted.

Financial Analysis

Financial analysis is another application of analytical auditing. In this situation the term "auditing" is used in a very broad sense to encompass any situation where an individual is evaluating financial data for reasonableness. Obviously, this situation might encompass uses by nonfinancial auditors or individuals other than professional auditors. For example, an individual preparing or evaluating a financial plan might use analytical auditing to project or determine the reasonableness of elements in that financial plan.

ANALYTICAL AUDITING TECHNIQUES

Table 1.1 lists most of the analytical auditing techniques commonly used by auditors. It is important to note that although analytical auditing may be employed for a variety of uses or applications, the techniques or methods used do not necessarily differ among the applications. For example, ratio analysis may be employed in any of the four applications previously discussed. Of course, since the objectives of each of the four applications will necessarily differ somewhat, the way in which a method or technique is employed might differ somewhat from application to application.

The techniques in Table 1.1 are described as categories of activity that might by used by an auditor in practice. Some of the techniques might actually involve the use of other techniques from the table. For example, pre-

TABLE 1.1. Analytical Auditing Techniques.

TITLE OF TECHNIQUE	METHODS OF APPLICATION
A. Comparison of two points	A1. Percent change from prior year A2. Dollar change from prior year A3. Combination of percent and dollar changes from prior year
B. Simple reasonableness tests	B1. Indirect computation of balance using causal factors
C. Ratio analysis	C1. Comparison with prior year ratio C2. Comparison with industry ratio C3. Comparison with competitor's ratio
D. Common-size statements	D1. Comparison of with prior year common-size amount D2. Comparison with industry common-size amount
E. Simple Time Series Analysis	E1. Review of trend through inspection of graph E2. Calculation of average change over period of time (may use trend statements) E3. Weighted moving average
F. Financial Forecast	F1. Review of client prepared budget, variances, and explanations of differences F2. Auditor prepares forecast and analyzes significant differences
G. Statistical Time Series Analysis	G1. Regression Analysis G2. ARIMA (Box-Jenkins) Methodology
H. Statistical Models of Financial Relationships	H1. Regression Analysis H2. Other Mathematical Modeling Techniques

paration of a financial forecast might involve the use of simple time-series analysis, statistical time-series analysis, or statistical modeling. Also, some of the techniques may be sometimes combined in practice. An example of this would be plotting of ratios on a carry-forward schedule to facilitate a simple time-series analysis of the ratio.

EVIDENCE THEORY UNDERLYING ANALYTICAL AUDITING

Analytical auditing has sometimes been described as an evidence creation technique since it produces data that previously did not exist. This description is an attempt to differentiate it from traditional tests of details that essentially corroborate financial statement assertions by examination of evidence already in existence. This distinction is only partially true since auditor creative effort is necessary even with tests of details but, nevertheless, the distinction may be a useful way of helping to categorize analytical auditing.

Analytical auditing techniques have traditionally been labeled as "soft evidence" or "soft procedures" (Wallace Jan. 1983: 24-26). This categorization has occurred because the procedures typically had a high degree of subjectivity in implementation and interpretation. Also, many auditors have difficulty in deciding the evidential value of analytical auditing because it employs indirect techniques that involve modeling a relationship. "Soft evidence" may be contrasted with the "hard evidence" provided by traditional direct auditing techniques such as accounts receivable confirmation or inventory observation. These latter techniques were viewed as being fairly objective direct evidence and thus subject to a reasonably straightforward evaluation as evidence. These attitudes probably stem from the fact that analytical auditing initially only employed the first four techniques listed in Table 1.1. These methods are all older techniques that have been applied as highly subjective judgmental methods. The last four methods in Table 1.1 are newer methods that are more objective and, potentially at least, more effective.

The spiraling audit costs in the 1970's led to a search for more efficient and effective audit techniques. However, many auditors were reluctant to change traditional procedures despite criticisms such as the following which implicitly called for more analytical auditing and fewer traditional tests of details:

How long has it been since we have significantly changed the audit format? Are the same procedures that were used on much smaller clients twenty years ago still appropriate today? . . . In particular, why should we spend hours footing and ticking the detailed account balances of a giant conglomerate when it is impossible either to examine every transaction in detail or to compute the resulting net income exactly? Doesn't such an approach lead more to meaningless repetition than to a systematic review of the entire financial statement? (Albrecht 1977:48)

The inappropriate biases and old attitudes that some auditors had against analytical auditing gradually started to fade with new information about the effectiveness of this type of auditing. This information was being disseminated both from colleagues in practice and from research studies. In the first instance, practicing auditors informally passed along information to their colleagues about their success with analytical auditing. In the second instance, the results from various research studies, such as the Hylas and Ashton study, were gradually becoming general knowledge in auditing practice. Although several significant studies of analytical auditing effectiveness preceded the Hylas and Ashton study, this study was particularly significant because it made a fairly strong overall statement about analytical auditing generally. The study analyzed 281 errors requiring financial statement adjustments on 152 different audits by a national accounting firm. The authors found that a relatively large number of the errors (72 errors or 27% of the total errors) were initially signaled by analytical auditing techniques. Additionally, other "soft evidence" techniques, consisting of inquiry and expectations from prior years, signaled another large number of the errors (50 errors or 19% of the total errors). This means that forty-six percent of the total errors on the 152 different audits were initially signaled by "soft evidence" procedures (Hylas and Ashton 1982: 758). The Hylas and Ashton results were confirmed by a subsequent study by Biggs and Wild (1984) who surveyed practicing CPAs and found that analytical auditing procedures detected more than 40% of material errors.

It should be noted that even more recent research raises a caution in the use of analytical auditing: "Our findings appear to support the arguments of Willingham and others that analytical review may be good at spotting the presence of errors, but does not reliably indicate the absence of errors" (Loebbecke and Steinbart 1987: 87). This research was, however, based on annual data of very large industrial companies. It is unclear what similar research on less aggregated data for the same companies would reveal. Auditors would not normally use highly aggregated data as an audit test. The author believes that analytical auditing would be more effective in indicating the absence of errors when disaggregated data is used.

These previous research results about overall effectiveness, along with the results of earlier studies about the effectiveness of individual analytical audit procedures, have been significant enough to make even the most conservative auditor think about using analytical auditing to a greater degree.

Analytical auditing is used to generate evidence to prove or disprove a particular assertion such as an account balance reflecting a correct amount. Analytical auditing techniques constitute indirect support for a particular balance since they do not directly test the details underlying the balance. They should be based on the reasoning process similar to the one illustrated in Figure 1.1, Model of analytical auditing reasoning process. As illustrated in the left column of Figure 1.1, the client data is processed using one of the techniques described in Table 1.1 to obtain what we will call a "primary result." This processing may be initially done by the auditor, or as in the case of client prepared budget variance analysis, the processing may be done by the client. As illustrated in the right column of Figure 1.1, the auditor then normatively processes the data. Normative processing means the auditor processes the data using the same tech-

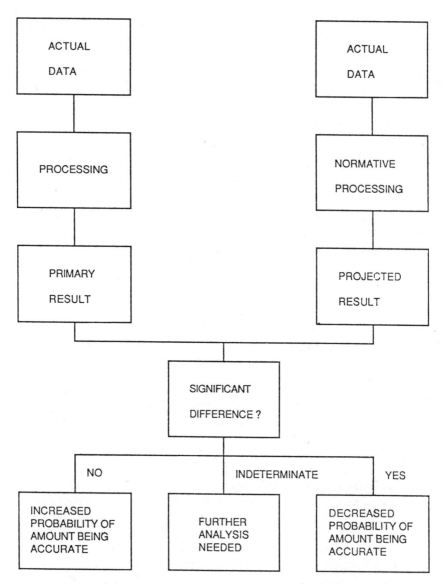

Figure 1.1. Model of analytical auditing reasoning process.

nique, but utilizing assumptions that the auditor deems appropriate for the auditor's projection, to obtain a "projected result." The actual result is then compared to the projected result to determine the degree of difference. An insignificant difference increases the probability of the data being accurate. A significant difference decreases the probability of the data being accurate. In some situations, the client may have previously computed both the actual and projected results, and the auditor will then have to, formally or informally, recompute the projected results. For example, assume the client prepared a budget for the current year and prepared an analysis of the difference between the actual accounting results and the budgeted accounting results (the budget variance). The auditor will either have to recompute the budget amounts or obtain adequate assurances about the client's budget preparation process in order to proceed with analytical auditing. The essence of analytical auditing is that the auditor prepares or appropriately uses a model to obtain projected results that can then be used by the auditor for comparative purposes.

The process described in Figure 1.1 can be somewhat iterative, i.e., the auditor may repeat it several times, since the key to the auditor projected results is the normative assumption upon which the projected result is based. An auditor may start with a set of tentative assumptions and may slightly vary them to see what the effect on the projected result and the related difference is before deciding on the final assumptions to be used. This process should not be used to manipulate the difference but rather as a means of evaluating the validity of the tentative assumptions. Since the costs associated with the decision outcomes could, either consciously or unconsciously, bias the auditor's selection of assumptions, it would normally be preferable to decide upon reasonable assumptions before commencing the analysis if this is possible.

Analytical auditing applications do not have to actually physically involve the parallel processing illustrated in Figure 1.1. An alternative is for the auditor to process data to obtain actual results and to only define what would constitute a significant difference if the normative processing had taken place. For example, an auditor may calculate the current year percentage change in a balance from the prior year and define a significant difference as being greater than a 12 percent change from the prior year. This might involve the assumption that 7 percent is a reasonable growth rate and the 5 percent is needed to allow for random fluctuations in the data. This process will achieve the same result as if the auditor had (1) calculated the actual percentage change from the prior year (actual result), (2) calculated a 7 percent increase from the prior year (projected result) and, (3) defined a significant difference as being greater than a 5 percent difference in the two results. This illustrates that it is possible to incorporate the effect of normative processing in the definition of the significant difference and avoid the actual second processing. Even though it is possible and sometimes desirable to not actually perform the parallel processing, the parallel processing model is extremely beneficial in helping auditors conceptualize what their actual reasoning process should be.

Figure 1.1 illustrates that the normal outcome of the analytical auditing process is to indicate either the increased or decreased probability that the financial statement amount is accurate. The acceptance or rejection of the financial statement amount depends on what other evidence is available in addition to the analytical auditing evidence. In order to prove a statement or proposition we must have, at a minimum, confirming evidence. Although a higher confidence criteria may be used, we will define confirming evidence as evidence that provides a .51 or greater confidence in the assertion or statement being true (renders the assertion more probable than not). This contrasts with supporting evidence which merely increases the probability of an assertion or statement being true but does not provide confirming evidence. Whether a particular analytical auditing technique produces confirming or supporting evidence depends on the probability of the proposition prior to the analytical auditing procedure being applied and the direction of the probability provided by the analytical auditing procedure. This concept may be illustrated by the following example:

Proposition Under Consideration	Recorded Amount of Repairs Expense Is Accurate
Probability of proposition prior to analytical auditing procedure	.34
Increase in probability of proposition resulting from analytical auditing procedure of comparison to industry percentage for account with no significant difference occurring	.11
Probability of proposition subsequent to analytical auditing procedure	.45
Conclusion	Analytical auditing procedure did not provide confirming evidence but merely supporting evidence.

If, in the previous example, the probability of the proposition prior to the analytical auditing procedure had been .40 or higher, the same procedure would have provided confirming evidence. This would occur because the prior probability of .40 would then have been combined with the probability from the analytical auditing procedure to produce a combined probability of .51.

The analytical auditing procedure could also have provided confirming evidence if it had provided an increase in the combined probability of .17 or higher. This would occur because the prior probability of .34 would then have been aggregated with the .17 or higher probability from the analytical auditing procedure to produce a combined probability of .51 or higher.

If we assume the auditor had foreknowledge of the .11 probability to be derived from the analytical auditing procedure in the example, and if confirming evidence was the objective of the procedure, then the auditor should have selected a more powerful procedure that would have provided a .17 or higher probability increase. Practicing auditors do not, of course, think in terms of exact probabilities from procedures but rather in terms of relative strengths of individual procedures in comparison to other procedures deemed possible.

INCREASED USE OF ANALYTICAL AUDITING

Economic, social, and competitive pressures have caused changes in audit practice over the last decades. Auditors have increased their search for effective and efficient ways to conduct audits. Some auditors have concluded that this means an increased reliance on analytical auditing procedures and less reliance on traditional direct tests where large amounts of individual transaction documentation is examined.

The increased importance of analytical auditing may be partially traced by reviewing the professional standards issued on the subject by the American Institute of CPAs. *Statement on Auditing Standards Number 23,* "Analytical Review Procedures," issued in 1978 was the first significant professional standard issued on this subject. Analytical auditing procedures were suggested but not formally required by this standard. Subsequent to that date, *Statement on Auditing Standards Number 36,* "Review of Interim Financial Information," and *Statement on Standards For Accounting and Review Services Number 1,* "Compilation and Review of Financial Statements," were issued. The latter two statements contained significant requirements for the use of analytical auditing. SAS 23 was replaced in 1988 by SAS 56 titled "Analytical Procedures" which formally required analytical auditing procedures in all financial audits. Thus we can see that in the last decade we have gone from no significant financial audit related professional standards on the subject to three major professional standards in the area.

Additional evidence about the increased importance of analytical auditing is provided by a research study conducted during the period 1978-1982 by Tabor and Willis. They analyzed the amount of analytical auditing employed in a sample of fourteen companies audited during

1978 and compared this to the amount of analytical auditing employed in the audits of the same companies in 1982. As illustrated in Table 1.2, Increase in Analytical Auditing, they found an average increase in use of analytical auditing of approximately 10% during that period.

The end of the Tabor and Willis study, 1982, corresponds approx-

TABLE 1.2. Increase in Analytical Auditing

	Changes in the Use of ARPs - 1978 to 1982 — By Audit Area —								
	PLANNING			DETAILED SUBSTANTIVE			FINAL REVIEW		
CLIENT	1978 (%)	1982 (%)	CHANGE (%)	1978 (%)	1982 (%)	CHANGE (%)	1978 (%)	1982 (%)	CHANGE (%)
1	88	90	+ 2	17	44	+ 27	11	10	- 1
2	89	91	+ 2	37	33	- 4	0	0	0
3	0	9	+ 9	29	18	- 11	0	0	0
4	0	0	0	25	31	+ 6	0	0	0
5	67	90	+ 23	17	34	+ 17	0	0	0
6	80	55	- 25	10	27	+ 17	0	0	0
7	8	22	+ 14	7	20	+ 13	0	5	+ 5
8	13	11	- 2	10	15	+ 5	0	5	+ 5
9	29	30	+ 1	26	29	+ 3	5	15	+ 10
10	22	26	+ 4	17	25	+ 8	11	10	- 1
11	0	0	0	54	65	+ 11	0	0	0
12	0	0	0	46	43	- 3	0	0	0
13	50	80	+ 30	29	58	+ 29	0	0	0
14	52	87	+ 35	26	63	+ 37	0	0	0
Average Diff.			+ 6.6			+ 10.5		[Too Few Data]	
t-Statistic (*)			1.6			2.8			
Significance Level (*)			(.10)			(.01)			

(*) For a paired sample t-test with a null hypothesis of
H_0: Av. Diff. = 0 and the alternative hypothesis of
H_a: Av. Diff. $>$ 0, because of an expectation of increased use of ARPs by audit area for 1982.

NOTE: Percentages are determined by dividing analytical review hours for the area by total audit hours for the respective area.

Source: R.H. Tabor and J.T. Willis. "Empirical Evidence On The Changing Role Of Analytical Review Procedures," AUDITING: A JOURNAL OF PRACTICE AND THEORY (Spring, 1985): 105. Reprinted with permission.

imately with another event that has been and continues to dramatically change traditional auditing, the advent of widespread microcomputer use in audit practice. In the short time period since 1982, microcomputers have gone from being rarely used on audits to a very common form of audit tool. Microcomputer audit software has also evolved during this same period. Many types of electronic working paper software packages now include traditional analytical auditing techniques such as simple trend analysis or ratio analysis as a standard feature. This means that it is easier than ever to use these techniques. Although there are no recent empirical studies comparable to the Tabor and Willis study to confirm this fact, we believe that the use of analytical auditing has increased even more sharply since 1982.

It is important not to overlook the fact that different analytical techniques are not employed with the same level of frequency in audit practice. In fact, the current state of practice is probably accurately summarized by the following comments; "Several basic analytical procedures are applicable in most practice settings and generally are applied in an extensive fashion. More exotic procedures requiring extensive mathematical techniques or additional data generation are only rarely employed in either audits or reviews" (Daroca and Holder 1985: 92). The current condition may change rapidly in the future. Factors influencing this change are (1) increased academic training of new auditors in advanced mathematical techniques, (2) the increased practicality of the advanced mathematical techniques due to microcomputer decision support systems, and (3) the increasing importance (perhaps even necessity) of analytical auditing techniques as audit tools in future advanced accounting information systems.

Another factor that will influence the future use of advanced analytical auditing techniques is that they may actually improve the audit process since they involve a more objective approach to auditing. The following comment provides a summary of this line of reasoning:

I would like to tell you what I think are some of the practical benefits of regression analysis, either in a limited review or in an audit.

- First, in the limited review and in the audit, we obtain a much more disciplined approach to analytical review. . . .
- Second, regression forces the auditor to document. . . .
- Third, regression forces the auditor to really understand the business, not just check the numbers. . . .
- Fourth, in the long run, time will be saved.

(Akresh and Wallace 1982: 153)

AUTOMATION ISSUES

As discussed in the preceding paragraph, one of the factors which has accelerated the trend toward use of analytical auditing techniques is the increasing degree of audit automation. The following four significant types of audit automation have occurred to date:

Starting Time Period	Type of Audit Automation
1. Ancient Times	Manual numeric devices (e.g., abacus)
2. 1800's	Mechanical numeric devices (e.g., mechanical calculator)
3. 1960's	Electronic numeric devices (e.g., electronic calculators and computers)
4. 1980's	Artificial intelligence applications (e.g., expert systems for analytical review)

(Adapted from McKee 1986: 42-43. Reprinted with permission by *The CPA Journal*, July 1986, copyright 1986.)

The first two types of audit automation did not have a significant impact on analytical auditing. Use of electronic numeric devices was the first type of audit automation to have a significant impact on analytical auditing. Starting in the late 1960's some audit firms began to automate the computational part of analytical auditing through the use of time-sharing terminals connected to large computers. This use gradually increased until about 1982 when, as previously noted, microcomputers began to spread into auditing in a significant fashion. Microcomputer software packages now account for a very significant part of this type of automation. An example of the automation of the computation part of analytical auditing via microcomputer software may be seen in Table 1.3, Account Balance Comparison Example.

The most recent type of audit automation to have an impact on analytical auditing has been the development of expert systems technology. In simplest terms, an expert system may be defined as computer software that contains both the reasoning schemes and knowledge of experts in a particular area. The software can, therefore, make decisions that approximate a human expert. This means the computer software can, on the most advanced end, perform tasks that would otherwise require an expert or, on a less advanced level, provide advice to individuals as to what an expert would do in a particular set of circumstances. The obvious advantage of this type of technology is that computer software can do more than merely automate the computations or mechanical part of either an accounting information system or its related audit. With regard to the audit, the com-

TABLE 1.3. Account Balance Comparison Example.

REPORT DATE: 02/25/87
PREPARED BY :
Smith & Jones, CPAs
INDEX: 0400 TYPE: X CLASS: 0510

Example Client Company
December 31, 1986
ACCOUNT BALANCE COMPARISON (Lead schedule format)
General and Administrative Expenses

ACCOUNT	DESCRIPTION	PRIOR YEAR BALANCE	CURRENT YEAR ADJ. BALANCE	DIFFERENCE	PERCENT CHANGE
501	Accounting Fees	5,000.00	6,000.00	1,000.00	20.00%
503	Amortization	482.00	482.00	0.00	0.00%
504	Automobile Expense	3,822.65	6,547.35	2,724.70	71.27%
508	Bad Debt Expense	26.66	253.95	227.29	852.55%
512	Contributions	400.00	350.00	-50.00	-12.50%
514	Depreciation Expense	2,388.62	5,198.00	2,809.38	117.61%
519	Franchise Fees	10,000.00	22,300.00	12,300.00	123.00%
520	Insurance - Employees	1,200.00	1,500.00	300.00	25.00%
524	Insurance - Property	1,500.00	2,354.00	854.00	56.93%
526	Interest Expense	1,439.23	7,612.00	6,172.77	428.89%
530	Licenses and Fees	200.00	450.00	250.00	125.00%
534	Maintenance and Repairs	3,847.04	2,465.40	-1,381.64	-35.91%
536	Miscellaneous Expense	2,873.12	1,425.00	-1,448.12	-50.40%
540	Office Expense	729.21	578.45	-150.76	-20.67%
550	Rent Expense	12,000.00	15,000.00	3,000.00	25.00%
560	Salaries - Officers	80,000.00	120,000.00	40,000.00	50.00%
562	Salaries and Wages - Other	64,039.00	78,534.00	14,495.00	22.63%
564	Supplies Expense	746.98	985.80	238.82	31.97%
570	Taxes - Payroll	10,317.45	14,325.76	4,008.31	38.85%
572	Taxes - Property	2,634.00	3,645.20	1,011.20	38.39%
TOTAL: General and Administrative Expenses		203,645.96	290,006.91	86,360.95	42.40%

Source: Financial Audit Systems. Field Audit System Technology Sample Reports. Raleigh: Financial Audit Systems, 1987, page 25. Reprinted with permission.

TABLE 1.4. Expert System Comments Report.

```
REPORT DATE: 11/30/85 09:35          COMMENTS REPORT              PAGE   1
PREPARED BY:                       Acme Widgets, Inc.
REVIEWED BY:                         June 30, 1985
-------------------------------------------------------------------------

   COMMENT NO.                      COMMENTS
-------------------------------------------------------------------------

        1     This could represent a problem with uncollectable
              receivable balances.

        2     This could result from possible misclassified or unrecorded
              cash sales, or overstated (possibly fictitious) credit
              sales.

        3     This could reflect inadequate management of accounts
              receivable, or weak or improperly implemented credit
              policies.

        4     Sales may have been recognized after the shipment but before
              the customer had agreed to pay.

        5     This could represent positive or improved receivables
              management.

        6     This could result from possible misclassified or unrecorded
              credit sales, or overstated (possibly fictitious) cash
              sales.

        7     This could represent possible cutoff problems (i.e. sales
              recorded but customers not yet billed).

        8     This could reflect improper use of credit memos or
              unauthorized write-offs.

        9     This could reflect possible cutoff problems. Could cost of
              sales be properly stated while credit sales are understated?

       10     This could reflect possible cutoff problems.  Could cost of
              sales be properly stated while credit sales are overstated?

       11     This could result from misclassified or fictitious credit
              sales.

       12     Are A/R write-offs and the allowance account being accounted
              for consistently from year to year?
```

Report 343 - Comments Report

Source: Financial Audit Systems. Answers User Guide. Raleigh: Financial Audit Systems, 1987, page 340.11. Reprinted with permission.

puter software can either perform or assist in performing the reasoning part of audit procedures. For example, there is currently expert analytical auditing software that can calculate financial ratios, interpret the results, and provide comments for the user as to possible significance of any deviations noted. An example of a comment report produced by an expert system is provided in Table 1.4, Expert System Comments Report.

Continued increases in audit automation make it easier and more cost-effective to employ analytical auditing procedures of all types. Given the effectiveness of analytical auditing techniques, this means that we will continue to witness dramatic increases in the use of analytical auditing.

The remainder of this book is devoted to a detailed examination of various analytical auditing techniques and how they relate to current professional auditing. Chapter 2 contains a detailed description of the methodology of the analytical auditing process. Chapter 3 reviews both the current professional standards impacting on analytical auditing and the use of analytical auditing in audit risk identification and control. Chapters 4 through 10 describe and illustrate analytical auditing techniques starting with the simplest techniques and finishing with the most advanced techniques currently being used in audit practice today.

REFERENCES

Akresh, A.D., and W.A. Wallace. "The Application of Regression Analysis for Limited Review and Audit Planning," *Symposium on Auditing Research IV,* Audit Group at the University of Illinois at Urbana-Champaign, 1982, 67-128, 147-161.

Albrecht, W. "Toward Better and More Efficient Audits," *Journal of Accountancy* (December 1977): 48-50.

American Institute of Certified Public Accountants. *Professional Standards,* Volumes 1 and 2. New York: AICPA, 1987.

Biggs, S. F., and J.J. Wild. "A Note on the Practice of Analytical Review," *Auditing: A Journal of Practice and Theory* (Spring 1984): 68-79.

Blocher, E., and J. J. Willingham. *Analytical Review- A Guide to Evaluating Financial Statements.* New York: McGraw Hill Book Company, 1985.

Blocher, E. "Approaching Analytical Review," *The CPA Journal* (March 1983): 24-32.

Casler, D. J., and J. R. Crockett. *Operational Auditing: An Introduction.* Altamonte Springs, Florida: The Institute of Internal Auditors, 1982.

Daroca, F. P., and W. W. Holder. "The Use of Analytical Procedures in Review and Audit Engagements," *Auditing: A Journal of Practice and Theory* (Spring 1985): 80-92.

Financial Audit Systems. *Answers User Guide.* Raleigh, North Carolina: Financial Audit Systems, 1987.

Financial Audit Systems. *Field Audit System Technology Sample Reports.* Raleigh, North Carolina: Financial Audit Systems, 1987.

Hylas, R. E., and R. H. Ashton. "Audit Detection of Financial Statement Errors," *The Accounting Review* (October 1982): 751-765.

Kissinger, J. N. "A General Theory of Evidence as the Conceptual Foundation in Auditing Theory: Some Comments and Extensions," *The Accounting Review* (April 1977): 322-339.

Loebbecke, J. K., and P. J. Steinbart. "An Investigation of the Use of Preliminary Analytical Review to Provide Substantive Audit Evidence," *Auditing: A Journal of Practice and Theory* (Spring 1987): 74-89.

McKee, T. E. "Does Your Practice Have a Place for an Expert System?" *The CPA Journal* (January 1988): 114-119.

McKee, T. E. *Analytical Techniques for Audit or Review Purposes* (CPA coursebook). New York: American Institute of Certified Public Accountants, 1987.

McKee, T. E. "Expert Systems: The Final Frontier?," *The CPA Journal* (July 1986): 42-46.

McKee, T. E. "Developments in Analytical Review," *The CPA Journal* (January 1982): 36-42.

Smith, D. G. *Analytical Review—A Research Study.* Canada: The Canadian Institute of Chartered Accountants, 1983.

Tabor, R. H., and J. T. Willis. "Empirical Evidence on the Changing Role of Analytical Review Procedures," *Auditing: A Journal of Practice and Theory* (Spring 1985): 93-109.

Toba, Y. "A General Theory of Evidence as the Conceptual Foundation in Auditing Theory," *The Accounting Review* (January 1975): 7-24.

Toba, Y. "A Semantic Meaning Analysis of the Ultimate Proposition to be Verified by Independent Auditors," *The Accounting Review* (October 1980): 604-619.

Wallace, W. A. "Analytical Review: Misconceptions, Applications and Experience —Part I," *The CPA Journal* (January 1983): 24-37.

Wallace, W. A. "Analytical Review: Misconceptions, Applications and Experience —Part II," *The CPA Journal* (February 1983): 18-27.

Westwick, C. A. *Do the Figures Make Sense?—A Practical Guide to Analytical Review.* England: The Institute of Chartered Accountants in England and Wales, 1981.

2
The Analytical Auditing Process

An individual audit or attestation engagement may be viewed as a complex series of interrelated evidence gathering and evaluating procedures. Analytical auditing is frequently only one of many potential procedures for an auditor to consider choosing. The decision to choose a specific analytical auditing technique is compounded by several factors. The auditor must consider items such as the state of knowledge about the audit entity, probable characteristics of the available data set, the efficiency and effectiveness of other possible audit techniques, the efficiency and effectiveness of various possible different analytical auditing techniques, and the degree and type of risk faced. Another factor compounding the decision process is that the auditor must also consider the relative strength of the analytical auditing evidence needed.

If analytical auditing is to be used merely as an "attention directing" technique (Kinney 1979:149) to identify areas where audit testing is needed, then "strong" evidence is not necessarily needed since the additional audit testing would be the primary means of controlling audit risk from the specific account or area. Of course, misdirected audit testing could result in overall audit inefficiencies and ineffectiveness so analytical auditing techniques must have a reasonable degree of reliability. When analytical auditing is used as a "primary evidence" procedure or "test-of-details-substitute" in support of an account then "strong" evidence may be needed if there are no other planned procedures for the account. The auditor would consider the evidence concepts of "supporting" evidence and "confirming" evidence discussed in the previous chapter. The auditor must evaluate all the factors previously discussed and make some practical decisions about how to conduct the audit.

This chapter provides a framework or process that is very useful in understanding and appropriately applying analytical auditing. Although there are certainly other possible approaches, the process presented will enable auditors to better understand and deal with potential problems in applying analytical auditing. This process can help an auditor answer the following questions:

- *When* should analytical auditing be employed?
- *What* considerations should influence the selection of an analytical auditing technique?
- *How* should the final decision criteria be determined?
- *What* decision methodology should be used to evaluate the results of analytical auditing procedures?

The process discussed in this chapter is applied in the context of a financial audit. Space limitations preclude a full discussion in the context of other types of audits although some comments on such applications are made.

THE ANALYTICAL AUDIT PROCESS

The analytical auditing process may be described as satisfactory completion of the following ten specific steps:

Step 1. Evaluation of specific risk factors.
Step 2. Determination if evidence is needed to reduce risk factors.
Step 3. Determination if analytical auditing could provide appropriate evidence.
Step 4. Selection of a specific analytical auditing procedure.
Step 5. Determination of what will constitute a material difference in applying the analytical auditing procedure.
Step 6. Application of the analytical auditing procedure and calculation of the actual result.
Step 7. Application of the analytical procedure and calculation of the projected result.
Step 8. Deciding if the actual result is materially different from the projected result. Investigating material differences when appropriate.
Step 9. Appropriately adjusting evidence probabilities with respect to the assertion or assertions being evaluated.
Step 10. Integration of all evidence sources before arriving at a final decision.

In order to apply the ten steps appropriately the auditor needs three general types of knowledge: business knowledge, accounting knowledge, and analytical auditing knowledge. Business knowledge is required in order to understand the economic environment and the client's operations in that environment. Accounting knowledge is required in order to understand the nature of the relationships between financial and non-financial data. Analytical auditing knowledge is required in order to know under what circumstances analytical auditing is most appropriate and how to properly perform and evaluate analytical auditing procedures.

Although each step in the analytical auditing process will receive a detailed explanation and illustration in the remaining sections of this chapter, Table 2.1, Simplified Illustration of Analytical Audit Process, presents a simplified overview description of how the ten steps could be applied in auditing a single account.

EVALUATE SPECIFIC RISK FACTORS

Audits involve the accumulation of evidence to prove assertions. In normal audits the degree of proof required is significantly less than 100 percent confidence. This means that there is potentially a risk that the audit conclusion could be wrong. Every normal audit involves, therefore, at least two general types of risk. One type is the risk of incorrect rejection. The second risk is the risk of incorrect acceptance.

The risk of incorrect rejection would be realized when audit evidence leads the auditor to reject a balance (in a financial audit), a procedure (in a compliance audit), or a process (in an operational audit) that should be accepted. If the auditor performs other audit procedures that indicate the correct decision, this risk has primarily efficiency significance. If, however, the auditor does not perform other procedures that indicate the correct decision, or if the wrong decision leads the auditor to use other procedures that lead the auditor to wrong conclusions in other areas of the audit, then this risk has effectiveness implications.

The risk of incorrect acceptance would be realized when the audit evidence leads the auditor to accept a balance, procedure, or process that the auditor should reject. This risk normally only affects the effectiveness of the audit since other procedures would not be performed as a result of the test. This risk is usually more significant than the risk of incorrect rejection since an audit failure could occur if other planned procedures did not alert the auditor to the incorrect balance, procedure, or process.

An auditor can only evaluate the consequences of the risks of incorrect acceptance or rejection with regard to the specific assertion being evaluated and the assertion's significance to the specific type of audit. Therefore, risk evaluation must be done in the framework of a specific audit and

TABLE 2.1. Simplified Illustration of Analytical Audit Process.

Assume the analytical audit process will be applied as a substantive test of a revenue account in the financial audit of a small service business.

STEP QUESTION	DESCRIPTION
1. Risk Factors?	Auditor concludes that there is significant risk that completeness assertion could be violated since owner could understate revenues to avoid income taxes.
2. Evidence Needed?	Yes, since no reliance can be placed on internal control system and observation and inquiry about revenue recording are only other related completed procedures.
3. Analytical Auditing Appropriate?	Yes, analytical procedure should provide confirming evidence in conjunction with planned accounts receivable confirmation procedures.
4. Specific Procedure?	Simple trend analysis should be a strong enough procedure based on stable nature of industry and planned year-end confirmation of receivables.
5. Material Difference?	$ 10,000 based on allocated tolerable error for account.
6. Actual Result?	Recorded revenue for current year was $ 600,000.
7. Projected Result?	Prior year revenue of $ 520,000 increased by projected industry revenue increase of 16%, projects to $ 603,200 ($ 520,000 x 1.16 = $ 603,200)
8. Actual Result Differ From Projected Result By More Than Material Difference?	No. Projected result ($ 603,200) differs from actual result ($ 600,000) by only $ 3,200 which is less than specified material difference of $ 10,000.
9. Adjust Evidence Probabilities	Closeness of results and strength of procedure provides significantly increased probability that all revenues are recorded.
10. Integrate Other Evidence In Final Decision.	Final acceptance of completeness assertion with respect to revenue account depends on appropriately positive evidence from accounts receivable confirmations.

individual account assertions in order to be meaningful. The following list contains five common assertions that are ordinarily evaluated by an auditor for each financial statement category (AICPA 1987: AU Section 326):

1. Completeness. All transactions and accounts that should be presented in the financial statements are included.
2. Valuation or allocation. Accounts have been included in the financial statements at appropriate amounts as determined by generally accepted accounting principles.
3. Existence or occurrence. Assets and liabilities exist at the financial statement date and transactions occurred during the period reported on.
4. Rights and obligations. Assets are the rights of the entity and liabilities are the obligations of the entity at the financial statement date.
5. Presentation and disclosure. Components of the financial statements are properly classified, described, and disclosed as determined by generally accepted accounting principles.

An additional assertion is used by some auditors. Other auditors include this assertion as part of the existence assertion.

6. Statement source (clerical accuracy). The financial statement amounts are a product of the entity's accounting information system.

It is important for auditors to remember that specific audit tests on a single account, including analytical auditing procedures, may only provide evidence with respect to one or a few of these assertions for that account. Other tests may be necessary with respect to the remaining assertions for that account.

We are going to analyze the analytical auditing process by examining the use of analytical auditing at different phases of a typical financial audit conducted by an external independent auditor in accordance with generally accepted auditing standards (GAAS). Figure 2.1, Flowchart of the audit process, provides a detailed model within which we can evaluate such an audit.

One potential use of analytical auditing would be a client acceptance or continuance decision which occurs at point (1.1) in Figure 2.1. Two specific risk factors associated with this decision would include the risk of possible regulatory sanctions and the risk of bankruptcy. If either of these risks were actually realized, an external auditor associated with such a client could suffer a direct loss through an event such as litigation or an indirect loss caused by bad publicity. The professional literature contains

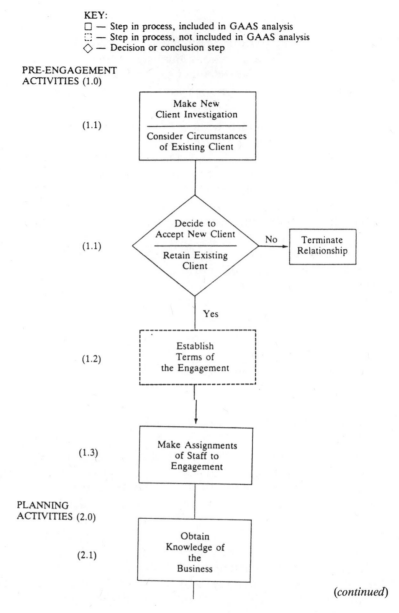

KEY:
□ — Step in process, included in GAAS analysis
⊡ — Step in process, not included in GAAS analysis
◇ — Decision or conclusion step

PRE-ENGAGEMENT
ACTIVITIES (1.0)

(1.1)
Make New
Client Investigation
—————————
Consider Circumstances
of Existing Client

(1.1)
Decide to
Accept New Client
—————————
Retain Existing
Client

No → Terminate Relationship

Yes

(1.2)
Establish
Terms of
the Engagement

(1.3)
Make Assignments
of Staff to
Engagement

PLANNING
ACTIVITIES (2.0)

(2.1)
Obtain
Knowledge of
the
Business

(continued)

Figure 2.1. Flowchart of the audit process.

Source: B.E. Cushing and J.K. Loebbecke. "Comparison of Audit Methodologies of Large Accounting Firms" [Studies in Accounting Research No. 26]. American Accounting Association, 1986, pages 7-12. Reprinted with permission.

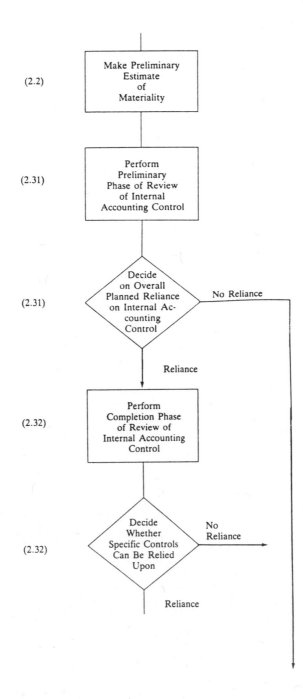

Figure 2.1. (*Continued*).

25

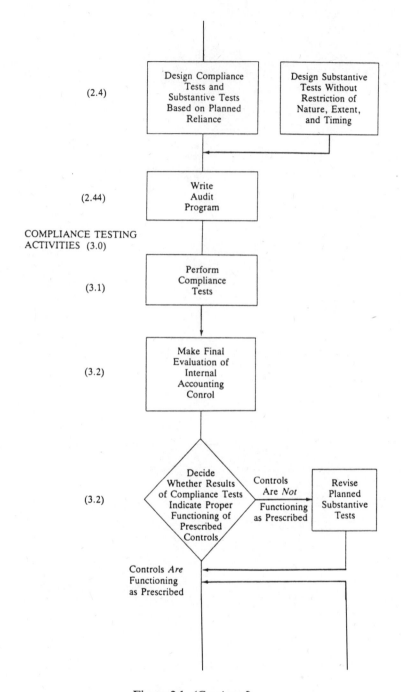

(2.4)

(2.44)

COMPLIANCE TESTING
ACTIVITIES (3.0)

(3.1)

(3.2)

(3.2)

Design Compliance
Tests and
Substantive Tests
Based on Planned
Reliance

Design Substantive
Tests Without
Restriction of
Nature, Extent,
and Timing

Write
Audit
Program

Perform
Compliance
Tests

Make Final
Evaluation of
Internal
Accounting
Control

Decide
Whether Results
of Compliance Tests
Indicate Proper
Functioning of
Prescribed
Controls

Controls
Are *Not*
Functioning
as Prescribed

Revise
Planned
Substantive
Tests

Controls *Are*
Functioning
as Prescribed

Figure 2.1. (*Continued*).

26

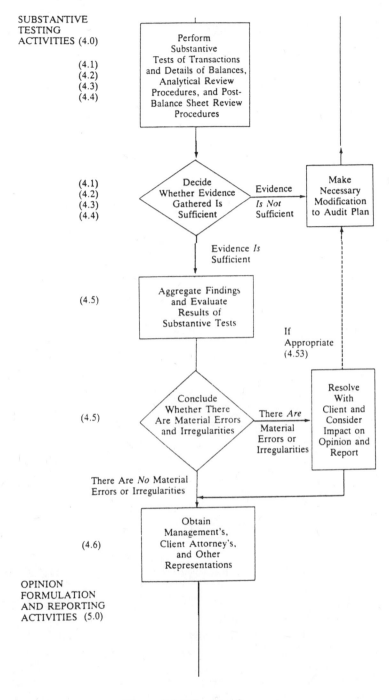

SUBSTANTIVE
TESTING
ACTIVITIES (4.0)

(4.1)
(4.2)
(4.3)
(4.4)

Perform
Substantive
Tests of Transactions
and Details of Balances,
Analytical Review
Procedures, and Post-
Balance Sheet Review
Procedures

(4.1)
(4.2)
(4.3)
(4.4)

Decide
Whether Evidence
Gathered Is
Sufficient

Evidence
Is Not
Sufficient

Make
Necessary
Modification
to Audit Plan

Evidence *Is*
Sufficient

(4.5)

Aggregate Findings
and Evaluate
Results of
Substantive Tests

If
Appropriate
(4.53)

(4.5)

Conclude
Whether There
Are Material Errors
and Irregularities

There *Are*
Material
Errors or
Irregularities

Resolve
With
Client and
Consider
Impact on
Opinion and
Report

There Are *No* Material
Errors or Irregularities

(4.6)

Obtain
Management's,
Client Attorney's,
and Other
Representations

OPINION
FORMULATION
AND REPORTING
ACTIVITIES (5.0)

Figure 2.1. (*Continued*).

27

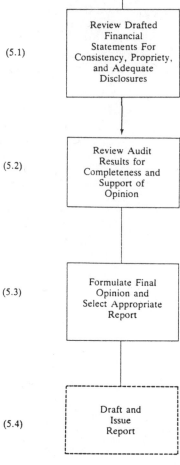

(5.1)

Review Drafted
Financial
Statements For
Consistency, Propriety,
and Adequate
Disclosures

(5.2)

Review Audit
Results for
Completeness and
Support of
Opinion

(5.3)

Formulate Final
Opinion and
Select Appropriate
Report

(5.4)

Draft and
Issue
Report

Figure 2.1. (*Continued*).

examples of other risk factors that should be considered at this stage in the audit.

A second potential use of analytical auditing is in obtaining an appropriate knowledge to plan an audit strategy. The audit planning process occurs at point (2.1) in Figure 2.1. Analytical auditing assists in this by helping the auditor to (1) obtain an appropriate knowledge of the business and industry, (2) identify potential financial and operational weaknesses, and (3) to identify accounts with significant fluctuations that warrant further audit investigation. This knowledge assists in determining the nature, extent, and timing of audit tests. An audit that is appropriately planned using analytical auditing may be compared to a "rifle" approach rather than a "shotgun" approach to auditing in that it focuses audit effort more precisely on those areas of greatest risk to the auditor. There are a wide variety of specific risks which the auditor might address at this stage of the audit. For example, the auditor might want to evaluate the risk of excess or obsolete inventory. If the risk is high the auditor may want to use stronger inventory audit procedures and/or allocate more time in the inventory area of the audit.

A third potential use of analytical auditing is as a substantive testing activity to provide appropriate evidence with respect to various accounts. This type of use occurs at point (4.2) in Figure 2.1. The risks here are, obviously, that the accounts might be materially misstated. Table 2.1 provided an abbreviated example of this type of use. A different application from that illustrated in Table 2.1 might be when the auditor wants to evaluate the risk of overstatement for a large number of relatively small expense accounts. If analytical procedures indicate no significant overstatements the auditor may avoid testing via a test of details comprising their balances.

The audit risks faced by an auditor conducting a financial audit of an individual account are summarized by the following formula adapted from the AICPA *Statements on Auditing Standards:*

Audit Risk = Inherent Risk × Control Risk × Detection Risk.

Audit risk is, of course, the risk that a material misstatement might remain in the financial statements after completion of the audit. It is the product or result of the other three risks. Inherent risk is risk of error or irregularity due to the nature of the account. Some accounts, such as marketable securities, are inherently more risky than other accounts, such as land, due to factors such as increased marketability. Control risk is the risk that the system of internal control will not prevent or detect errors on a timely basis. Detection risk is the risk that the auditors' planned tests, other than tests of the internal control system, will not detect any errors or irregularities that do occur. Each planned substantive audit test for an account helps reduce this risk if the test results are positive. Since analytical auditing procedures are one of two general classes of substantive tests, these procedures directly contribute to reducing the detection risk to an acceptable level. Figure 2.2, Audit risk diagram, depicts the relationships just discussed.

The final potential use of analytical auditing in the typical financial audit is in the final review of the overall financial statements at the completion of the audit. This occurs at point (5.1) in Figure 2.1. At this stage the auditor reviews the accounts after all potential adjustments have been booked or considered. The auditor is again concerned with the risk of material misstatement in the individual accounts but this assessment typically takes place at a later point in time than the previously discussed

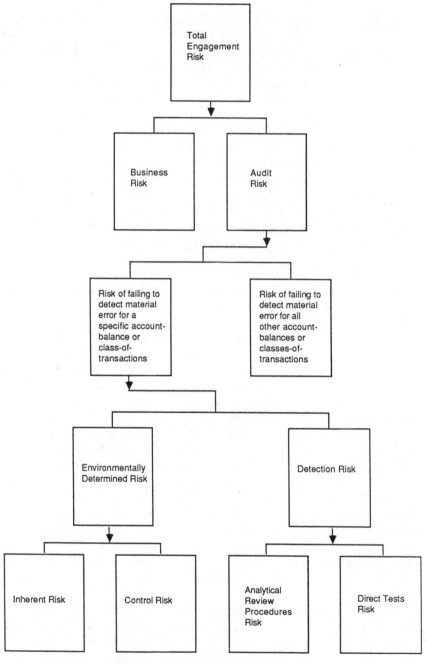

Figure 2.2. Audit risk diagram.

Source: T.E. McKee. "Materiality and Audit Risk." 1987: 2-10. Reprinted by permission.

substantive testing. Another risk that the auditor again considers at this stage in the audit is the risk of a going- concern problem.

It should be evident from the preceding discussion that an auditor must have a detailed knowledge of the audit process and specific analytical auditing procedures in order to know what risks are appropriate to consider and at what point in an audit that analytical auditing might be appropriate to help in assessing these risks. The audit or attestation model and potential uses would, of course, be different for other types of audits or attestation engagements. We will now examine steps 2 through 4 of the ten steps in analytical auditing process (Table 2.1). Our discussion will be focused on the client acceptance or continuance decision.

DETERMINE IF EVIDENCE IS NEEDED TO REDUCE RISK FACTORS

The second step in the analytical auditing process is to determine if the auditor needs evidence to reduce the risk factors to an acceptable level. The auditor would evaluate the significance of the possible adverse outcomes if the risk were actually realized. This would result in a decision as to whether further evidence were needed to appropriately evaluate the risk. Assume that an auditor decided further evidence was needed with respect to the risk of possible regulatory sanction and the risk of bankruptcy in the previously discussed client acceptance/continuance decision. The next step would be to determine if an analytical auditing procedure could provide that evidence.

DETERMINE IF ANALYTICAL AUDITING COULD PROVIDE APPROPRIATE EVIDENCE

Let us assume that the author knew of no analytical auditing technique that would provide evidence with respect to the risk of possible regulatory sanction. The auditor would, therefore, conclude that analytical auditing would not be appropriate in evaluating this risk.

Let us further assume that the auditor knew of two types of analytical auditing techniques that could provide strong evidence with regard to the risk of bankruptcy. These techniques could be financial ratio analysis and a mathematical modeling technique called discriminant analysis. The auditor would conclude that analytical auditing might be appropriate in evaluating this type of risk.

The auditor's decision at this stage of the analytical auditing process becomes a function of the auditor's knowledge of potential analytical auditing techniques. The more an auditor knows about specific analytical auditing techniques, the higher the probability the auditor could determine that such a technique would be appropriate to reduce the risk being considered. For example, let us reconsider the first risk addressed—the risk of regulatory sanction. Let us assume that the specific client being considered was a food service vendor and that, in the food service industry, ratios about product related injuries and sickness are very important. If fact, assume these ratios are a significant factor influencing a major client's decision to grant or deny a continuing franchise to the food service vendor. If this were true, and the auditor had knowledge of the significance of the injury and sickness ratios, then, the auditor might consider analytical auditing as a possible source of evidence about this risk.

SELECT A SPECIFIC ANALYTICAL AUDITING PROCEDURE

When there are two or more possible techniques, like ratio analysis and discriminant analysis, that bear on a specific risk such as bankruptcy, a good approach is to begin with the simplest technique that could provide the appropriate degree of evidence needed. Since, in our example, we merely want limited evidence about the possibility of bankruptcy, we might decide that ratio analysis would be adequate and the potentially more powerful technique of discriminant analysis would not be needed. We might also decide that a single ratio such as Cash Flow to Total Debt would be an adequate measure of the risk of bankruptcy for purposes of deciding whether we might want to accept a potential client. The Cash Flow to Total Debt ratio was found to be 87% accurate in classifying firms one year prior to bankruptcy. This accuracy only deteriorated to 78% even up to five years prior to bankruptcy (Beaver 1966: 85).

DETERMINE WHAT WILL CONSTITUTE A MATERIAL DIFFERENCE BEFORE APPLYING THE ANALYTICAL PROCEDURE

Auditing research has indicated that auditors may make poor decisions in some circumstances. One problem auditors have is that they may tend to excessively "anchor" their decisions in past data. This means that they frequently give too much weight to past data and do not always appropriately evaluate current evidence. For example, many continuing auditors assume a prior year audit program is appropriate for the current year with only minor modifications for conditions they identify as having changed from the prior year. This may be a poor assumption if the prior year audit program had efficiency or effectiveness problems that will be repeated because they are unrelated to any changing conditions which would cause the program to be modified. Another example involves sample size decisions. Evidence indicates auditors may select sample sizes which are overly influenced by the prior year sample size, effectively ignoring evidence that current year conditions call for a much different sample size.

Another potential problem with auditors' decisions is called "confirmation bias." This means that auditors have a tendency to favor or accept a hypothesis under consideration without adequately seeking out or considering disconfirming evidence or possible alternative hypotheses. For example, an auditor might accept a 10% increase in sales as being reasonable based on the fact that industry sales increased and the auditee's advertising expense increased. The auditor might not seek out or consider evidence about price reductions and production capacity limitations. Recent research indicates that experience may be an important factor in reducing confirmation bias (Biggs, Mock, and Watkins 1988: chap. 9, p. 18).

One way to overcome these potential problems with auditor's decisions is for the auditor to decide what will be a significant difference *before* constructing the actual models and calculating the difference between the projected result and the actual result. This approach forces the auditor to take a broad view of the analytical procedure which considers materiality, risk factors, financial data, operating data, and external data before getting involved with specific detailed information. The auditor may be, therefore, less likely to overlook other evidence or possible hypotheses. Also, since the auditor does not yet know the result of the test he or she will not be "biased" by the current test results when making a decision about whether the test results revealed something significant.

The determination of what constitutes a significant fluctuation will depend on a variety of factors such as materiality, tolerable error, confidence levels, direction of the test (overstatement or understatement), the strength of the analytical auditing procedure, and the variability of the data being examined. D.G. Smith comments on the difficulty in determining an appropriate amount:

Most practitioners find the determination of what constitutes a significant fluctuation or variation difficult. They suggest that determining the significance of fluctuations is a complex decision requiring a good deal of professional judgment, knowledge of the business and experience. The general consensus was that the auditor cannot use materiality as an absolute measure of the significance of fluctuations because of the differences in the nature and size of the populations being tested. As an example of this point, assume the following financial information and a materiality level of $10,000:

	Previous Year	Current Year	Increase
Sales	$1,000,000	$1,100,000	$100,000
Telephone Expense	10,000	15,000	5,000

Although the increase in sales exceeds materiality by 10 times, this increase may not be as unusual as the 50% increase in telephone expense, even though the increase of $5,000 is only half of materiality. Most practitioners indicated that, even though the $5,000 increase was not material, they would probably investigate the reason for the increase anyway (Smith 1983: 12). (Reprinted, with permission, from *Analytical Review,* 1983, published by The Canadian Institute of Chartered Accountants, Toronto, Canada.)

The preceding example illustrates the benefits of using a multiple criteria decision rule. Such a rule employs two or more criteria to arrive at a decision. A two criteria rule is sometimes called a "dual-screen" decision rule. This is a rule that employs two criteria to "screen" or sift out (determine) what might be material fluctuation. Such a rule in the proceeding example by D. G. Smith could have been to define a material fluctuation in an account as a fluctuation that exceeded either $10,000 (the materiality limit) or a 20% change from the prior year. Use of this rule would have caused both the sales and telephone expense accounts to have been investigated.

Let us continue with the example concerning evaluating the bankruptcy potential as part of the client acceptance/continuance decision. Assume that we consider, but reject, using a fixed cutoff point to signal when the ratio Cash Flow to Total Debt indicates a potential bankruptcy problem. We decide instead that it would be more appropriate to use the industry ratio of cash flow to debt to project what the company result should be and decide that a difference of 20% or more below the projected result will be a material difference.

APPLY THE ANALYTICAL PROCEDURE AND CALCULATE THE ACTUAL RESULT

In this step the auditor applies the analytical procedure to calculate the actual result for the company being audited. The auditor must be knowledgeable of the possible limitations and assumptions of the analytical procedure being employed. To continue the previous example assume the auditor calculates the ratio of cash flow to total debt for the potential client as being 1.6.

APPLY THE ANALYTICAL PROCEDURE AND CALCULATE THE PROJECTED RESULT

This is the step where the auditor applies the analytical procedure using the assumptions the auditor deems appropriate for the client being audited. The purpose of this step is to establish a normative result (theoretically acceptable result) against which to compare the actual result for the company. It is important to remember that there is no necessarily right or wrong answer derived from processing the company's data. The auditor simply produces data that has to be evaluated for reasonableness. The actual results (data) obtained from processing the client's actual data do not mean anything by themselves and only have meaning or significance when compared to a normative projected result as previously illustrated in Figure 1.1. To obtain results for comparison (normative results) auditors typically use one or more of the following data sources:

- Prior-period audited data
- Current industry statistics
- Historical industry statistics
- Client projections or budgets
- Data from related accounts or other internal data
- Rules of thumb
- Experience
- Trend extrapolations
- Statistical techniques

To continue with our previous example, let us assume that we decide that the industry cash flow to total debt ratio is the appropriate projected result. In other words, we decide that the company's ratio should at least equal the industry ratio. The industry ratio then becomes the normative (theoretically correct) amount. Assume that we consulted appropriate industry data and found that the industry cash flow to total debt ratio was 1.9.

DECIDE IF THE ACTUAL RESULT IS MATERIALLY DIFFERENT FROM THE PROJECTED RESULT

Step 8 should be a simple execution of the following decision rule: *Material Difference Exists if Projected Result (Step 7) minus Actual Result (Step 6) is greater than Materiality Amount or Rule (Step 5).*

In our continuing example, this rule would assume the following form:

Material Difference Exists if $1.9 - 1.6 >$ or $= .2 \times 1.9$
Material Difference Exists if $.3 \qquad >$ or $= .38$

Since the difference of .3, between the projected and actual results, was less than .38, we would conclude that no material difference exists.

If a material difference had occurred, the next question for the auditor would be, What could have caused the difference? In many circumstances the auditor has a professional responsibility to obtain an answer to this question.

An auditor considering a material difference would first normally consider his or her knowledge of the client and industry in attempting to explain the difference. If this were unsuccessful, then the auditor might ask a knowledgeable client official. A reasonable answer from an appropriate client official might be accepted outright. If the item is unusually significant, however, the auditor would also seek some type of corroborating evidence.

A potential problem is that due to inexperience or time pressure the auditor might stop investigating the difference before the actual cause is determined. An approach that might aid in preventing this problem is to work through the account balance implications of the proposed explanation:

Specifically, the auditor can make an "as if" entry to reverse the effect of the tentative explanation as if it were in fact correct. The auditor then conducts an analytical review of the tentatively revised numbers to see if important deviations still exist.

If the tentative explanation, in fact, is the correct explanation, then the revised analysis should yield fewer deviations from expectation than did the analysis using book values. On the other hand, if the explanation is incorrect, the revised ratios may exhibit even more unusual relationships than before (Kinney 1987: 69).

The normal possibilities for explanations are listed below with a brief explanation of each:

1. Change in underlying economic variables. The most common reason for significant differences is that some underlying economic variable has changed. For example, when an auditor seeks an explanation for a significant increase in the gross profit margin, he or she may find that management was able to increase prices significantly. The auditor should always remember that many accounting amounts are interrelated and ask if the change will affect other accounting numbers.
2. Omitted factor from model. It may be that the auditor overlooked a factor or variable which should have been used in calculating the projected result. If the auditor can ascertain that this occurred, then the auditor should make a new projection. One point at which an auditor may realize that something may have been omitted is when trying to determine what is an appropriate explanation for the material difference.
3. Change in accounting principle. A fairly infrequent explanation for a

significant difference is that the client changed accounting principles and the auditor was unaware of it.

4. Error. Another explanation is that the client made an unintentional error in recording data in the accounts. This cause is frequently not determinable without applying other auditing procedures to the account.

5. Irregularity. The most unwelcome explanation is that the client has intentionally misstated the account. This cause also normally requires other auditing procedures to determine whether it has occurred. When an auditor determines that an irregularity has taken place this changes the basic nature of the audit and the auditor must adopt a different posture for the remainder of the audit. If this condition appears to exist, auditors should review their responsibilities for dealing with irregularities as described by appropriate professional standards.

APPROPRIATELY ADJUST EVIDENCE PROBABILITIES WITH RESPECT TO ASSERTION BEING EVALUATED

To apply Step 9, the auditor considers solely the effect of the specific analytical procedure on the probability of the assertion being evaluated. As previously illustrated in Figure 1.1, this would usually result in one of three conclusions: (1) increased probability of assertion being true, (2) indeterminate result, so further analysis needed, or (3) decreased probability of assertion being true.

The amount of increase or decrease in the probability of the assertion being true is dependent on both the strength of the analytical procedure used and the significance of the difference obtained. Each of these factors must be evaluated by the auditor. Stronger analytical procedures will normally have a greater effect on the probability of an assertion being true than will weaker analytical procedures. Likewise, a difference much greater than the minimum difference the auditor deemed material may have a stronger effect on the auditor's evidence evaluation. There is obviously judgment involved in evaluating both these factors.

In our example, the difference of .3 was less than the .38 we specified as being material, so we would lower our assessment of the probability that the potential client might go bankrupt. Stated another way, the results of the analytical auditing procedure applied do not indicate a potential bankruptcy problem.

INTEGRATE ALL EVIDENCE SOURCES BEFORE ARRIVING AT A FINAL DECISION

The last step in the analytical auditing process is not actually a step that applies to a specific analytical auditing procedure. Rather it is more a reminder that in most cases analytical auditing only provides part of, not all, the information upon which auditors should base their decision. In most decision situations, an auditor has other data or information which should be considered in arriving at a final decision. This other information must be considered if the auditor is to make the "correct" decision.

To finish our continuing example, let us assume that the auditor also knows that the company's cash flow has improved for ten consecutive quarters and that the client's industry is forecasted to have excellent

TABLE 2.2. Error Evaluation Schedule.

Type of Error	Financial Statement Category	
	Balance Sheet Effect	Income Statement Effect
A. Unadjusted prior year errors with current year effect	$ 500	($ 500)
B. Unadjusted current year known errors	(2,000)	2,000
C. Unadjusted projected errors from sampling procedures	1,000	(1,000)
D. Potential undetected error in accounts tested solely via analytical auditing procedures:		
Account 1 times % [$ 4,000 x 50%]	(2,000)	2,000
Account 2 times % [$ 6,000 x 10%]	600	(600)
. . . .		
Account N times %		
Total Unadjusted Error	(1,900)	1,900
Less: Materiality Amount	5,000	5,000
Remaining Allowance for Undetected Error	$ 3,100	$ 3,100

growth for the next eighteen months. These additional pieces of information, along with the results of analytical auditing procedure, might lead an auditor to a final conclusion that the probability of bankruptcy is acceptably low.

One problem that the external independent financial auditor must deal with at this stage is the *Statement on Auditing Standards Number 47* requirement that the auditor aggregate all known and likely errors and then consider Potential Undetected Error, before making a final decision about an account or the overall financial statements. In audit practice, different

TABLE 2.3. Description of Analytical Auditing in Client Acceptance Decision.

The analytical audit process was applied to evaluate the bankruptcy potential of a possible new client.

STEP QUESTION	DESCRIPTION
1. Risk Factors?	Risk of client bankruptcy with related bad publicity or litigation.
2. Evidence Needed?	Yes, due to high potential costs if risks are actually realized.
3. Analytical Auditing Appropriate?	Yes, either ratio analysis or discriminant analysis could provide needed evidence.
4. Specific Procedure?	Ratio analysis. Specifically cash flow to total debt ratio.
5. Material Difference?	20% difference from industry ratio.
6. Actual Result?	Company cash flow to total debt ratio of 1.6.
7. Projected Result?	Industry cash flow to total debt ratio of 1.9.
8. Actual Result Differ From Projected Result More Than Material Difference?	Actual result of 1.6 differs from projected result of 1.9 by less than material difference of .38 [1.9 x 20% = .38].
9. Adjust Evidence Probabilities.	Analytical procedure indicates auditor should reduce risk assessment with respect to the client going bankrupt.
10. Integrate Other Evidence In Final Decision.	Improving company cash flow and strong industry growth along with results of analytical procedure lead auditor to conclude that risk of bankruptcy is acceptably low.

auditors employ different audit methodologies to accomplish this objective. One approach is an error aggregation and evaluation schedule which contains a line for accounts audited solely via analytical auditing procedures. These accounts have an appropriate percentage reserved for potential undetected error. The amount reserved is either positive or negative depending on the auditor's assessment of the most likely misstatement direction for the account. The appropriate percentage is a matter of judgment and depends on factors such as the inherent risk, control risk, and strength of the analytical auditing procedure applied to the account. The auditor sums known errors, likely errors, and potential errors in accounts audited solely via analytical auditing procedures. He or she then subtracts the financial statement materiality amount from this sum and judgmentally determines if the remaining allowance for undetected error is large enough considering the potential types of risks faced. If the remaining allowance for undetected error is not adequate, the auditor can suggest that the client adjust some of the known errors or projected errors and/or apply additional audit procedures to reduce the potential undetected error in accounts audited solely via analytical auditing procedures. Table 2.2, Error Evaluation Schedule, illustrates one possible form for such a schedule.

Most auditors would utilize columns reflecting less aggregated data in such a schedule. For example, instead of a single column for balance sheet effect, there may be columns for current asset effect, long-term asset effect, total asset effect, current liability effect, long-term liability effect, and shareholders's equity effect. These columns will permit the auditor to evaluate the effect on specific balance sheet components or on ratios, such as the current ratio.

Table 2.3, Description of Analytical Auditing in Client Acceptance Decision, summarizes the application of the previously discussed ten steps in the analytical auditing process as applied to our client acceptance example.

REFERENCES

American Institute of Certified Public Accountants. *Professional Standards,* Volumes 1 and 2. New York: AICPA, 1987.

Arrington, C. E., W. Hillison, and R. C. Icerman, "Research in Analytical Review: The State of the Art," *Journal of Accounting Literature* (1983): 151–185.

Beaver, W. "Financial Ratios as Predictors of Failure," *Journal of Accounting Research* (Supplement 1966): 71–111.

Biggs, S. F., T. J. Mock, and P. R. Watkins. *Analytical Review Procedures and Processes in Auditing* (Research Monograph No. 14). Toronto: Canadian Certified General Accountants Research Foundation, 1988.

Blocher, E., and J. J. Willingham, *Analytical Review—A Guide to Evaluating Financial Statements.* New York: McGraw-Hill Book Company, 1985.

Blocher, E. "Approaching Analytical Review," *The CPA Journal* (March 1983): 24–32.

Kinney, W. R. "Attention-Directing Analytical Review Using Accounting Ratios: A Case Study," *Auditing: A Journal of Practice & Theory* (Spring 1987): 59–73.

Kinney, W. R. "Quantitative Applications in Auditing," *Journal of Accounting Literature* (1983): 187–204.

Kinney, W. R. "The Predictive Power of Limited Information in Preliminary Analytical Review: An Empirical Study," *Journal of Accounting Research* (Vol. 17 supplement 1979): 148–165.

Smith, D. G. *Analytical Review—A Research Study.* Toronto: Canadian Institute of Chartered Accountants, 1983.

Westwick, C. A. *Do The Figures Make Sense? A Practical Guide to Analytical Review.* England: The Institute of Chartered Accountants in England and Wales, 1981.

3
Professional Standards and Audit Risk

Professional auditors strive to gather appropriate audit evidence at a reasonable time and expense, and comply with professional standards while doing so. Professional standards provide the framework for evaluating what is appropriate evidence and how it should be obtained. Consequently, they are of significance to auditors planning analytical auditing procedures. It is rather surprising, in view of the widespread use of analytical auditing in all types of attestation engagements, that there are few audit standards which contain explicit guidance about analytical auditing. In fact, there are only two audit standards (one U.S. and one international) that deal exclusively with analytical auditing and these are virtually identical. This chapter summarizes and interprets the different professional standards that relate to analytical auditing for both external independent auditors and internal auditors.

Audit risk is an important factor determining the type and amount of audit evidence. This chapter explains how audit risk analysis impacts on analytical auditing and provides some practical examples of how auditors may use audit risk analysis to help plan their analytical auditing procedures.

INTERNATIONAL AUDITING STANDARDS

The International Federation of Accountants was created in 1977 as a result of an agreement signed by 49 different countries including the United States of America. This organization issues auditing standards through its International Auditing Practices Committee (IAPC). The

IAPC establishes auditing standards through the issuance of both international auditing guidelines (IAG) and statements. The IAPC auditing standards are intended for worldwide acceptance but do not override auditing standards of countries who have local standards that may differ from the IAPC standards. Countries who have differing standards are encouraged to work toward harmony with the IAPC auditing standards.

International Auditing Guideline 3, originally issued in 1980, refers to analytical auditing in its discussion of audit evidence. It states "The auditor should obtain sufficient appropriate audit evidence through the performance of compliance and substantive procedures to enable him to draw reasonable conclusions therefrom on which to base his opinion on the financial information." It then proceeds to describe substantive procedures as consisting of the following two types:

- tests of details of transactions and balances;
- analysis of significant ratios and trends including the resulting investigation of unusual fluctuations and items. (IAPC 1987: 12,164–12,165).

Since the latter type of substantive audit procedure is clearly a description of analytical auditing, this early standard clearly established analytical auditing as one of the major classes of appropriate audit procedures.

International Auditing Guideline 8, issued in 1982, discusses audit evidence. It lists the financial statement assertions that an auditor might seek to validate via analytical auditing procedures as consisting of existence, rights and obligations, occurrence, valuation, measurement, and presentation and disclosure. It then reaffirms IAG3 by listing analytical review as one of the methods available to the auditor for verifying these assertions.

International Auditing Guideline 12 was issued in 1983 and titled "Analytical Review." It contains a brief discussion of some general aspects of analytical auditing. This guideline is very similar to the U.S. *Statement on Auditing Standards 23* "Analytical Review," now superseded, which was issued about five years previously. The major points are reviewed in our discussion of U.S. auditing standards.

International Auditing Guideline 16 was issued in 1984 and titled "Computer-Assisted Audit Techniques." It discusses techniques that use the computer as an audit tool. There is no comparable U.S. auditing standard. It lists various uses for computer assisted audit techniques (CAATs) including: "Analytical review procedures—for example, the use of audit software to identify unusual fluctuations or items" (IAPC 1987: 12,472). Examples of use of CAATs that may improve audit effectiveness and efficiency include: "In applying analytical review procedures, transactions or balance details may be reviewed and reports printed of unusual items more efficiently by using the computer than by manual methods" (IAPC

1987: 12,474). This IAG also requires auditors using CAATs to have a degree of knowledge sufficient to plan, execute, and use the results of the particular CAAT adopted. It contains a detailed listing of major steps to be undertaken and documentation required by auditors using CAATs.

International Auditing Guideline 23 was issued in 1986 and titled "Going Concern." It includes a list of fifteen possible indicators to a going concern problem that includes "Adverse key financial ratios," an analytical auditing procedure. Auditors are required to consider these indicators when planning and performing an audit. When it is determined that a going concern problem exists, the auditor has to consider additional disclosures and possible report modification. This standard is clearly more demanding than the U.S. auditing standard in effect when it was issued. The standard states that "when planning and performing audit procedures and in evaluating the results thereof, the auditor should be alert to the possibility that the going concern assumption on which the preparation of the financial statements is based may be subjected to question" (IAPC 1987: 12,568). This appears to place the auditor in an active role with respect to evaluating whether there is a going concern problem. Issued in 1988, the U.S. *Statement on Auditing Standards 59,* "The Auditor's Consideration of an Entity's Ability to Continue as a Going Concern," contains wording similar to the international standard. It states "The auditor has a responsibility to evaluate whether there is substantial doubt about the entity's ability to continue as a going concern for a reasonable period of time, not to exceed one year beyond the date of the financial statements being audited" (AICPA 1988: 2).

No other IAG directly discusses analytical auditing. The IAGs dealing with materiality, audit risk, audit sampling, fraud and error, and other matters contain indirect references to analytical auditing procedures. These requirements are similar to U.S. standards and will be discussed later in this chapter.

AMERICAN INSTITUTE OF CPAs PROFESSIONAL STANDARDS

The American Institute of Certified Public Accountants (AICPA) has been issuing auditing standards of various types since 1917. There are currently four different types of standards in effect which auditors may be concerned with:

- Statements on Standards for Attestation Engagements
- Statements on Auditing Standards
- Statements on Standards for Accounting and Review Services
- Statements on Standards for Accountants' Services on Prospective Financial Information

The Statements on Standards for Attestation Engagements (SSAEs) were first issued in 1986. They are intended to apply to all types of attest services including audits, reviews, compilations, and other limited assurance engagements. Being very new they may be in conflict with some older standards, accordingly they are not now intended to supersede any of the other standards. "An attest engagement is one in which a practitioner is engaged to issue or does issue a written communication that expresses a conclusion about the reliability of a written assertion that is the responsibility of another party" (AICPA 1987: vol. 1, 1511).

The Statements on Auditing Standards (SASs) were first issued in 1972. SAS Number 1 was a codification of prior Statements on Auditing Procedures. These standards apply to audit engagements. An audit opinion represents the highest level of assurance which can be rendered.

Statements on Standards for Accounting and Review Services (SSARs) were first issued in 1978. They apply to compilations, which provide a very low level of assurance, and to reviews which provide limited assurances. These statements greatly heightened the interest in analytical auditing since they included inquiries and analytical procedures as the two main evidence sources for review engagements. Review engagements have now become a substantial part of the practice of many CPAs thus fueling the growth in the use of analytical auditing. The analytical procedures which the SSARS discussed included: (1) comparison of the financial statements with statements for comparable prior period(s); (2) comparison of the financial statements with anticipated results, if available (for example, budgets and forecasts); and (3) study of the relationships of the elements of the financial statements that would be expected to conform to a predictable pattern based on the entity's experience. The SSARS standards are intended to apply only to engagements for private companies.

Statements on Standards for Accountants' Services on Prospective Financial Information (SSASPFI) were first issued in 1986. They provide guidance for engagements when a CPA is associated with forecasts, projections, or other prospective financial information. The SSASPFIs do not discuss analytical auditing directly. However, since analytical auditing procedures provide the basis for assurance about many projections and forecasts, auditors performing this type of attest engagement will want to be fully informed about analytical auditing.

We will only discuss the requirements of the SASs since they provide the most detailed information relating to the application of analytical auditing. The other standards contain only very limited guidance with respect to application of analytical auditing.

STATEMENTS ON AUDITING STANDARDS

"Analytical review first appeared in the professional standards of auditing in Statement on Auditing Procedure No. 54 in 1972." (Kinney 1979: 149)

Shortly after it was issued, this pronouncement was replaced by *Statement on Auditing Standards Number 1,* "Codification of Auditing Standards and Procedures." Analytical auditing was discussed in this pronouncement only to the extent of mentioning it and direct tests of detail of transactions and balances as comprising the two major classes of substantive testing. This discussion, however, reflected a long standing usage of analytical auditing by auditors. "For example, reference to analytical review procedures appears in a 1935 (Deloitte) Haskins & Sells audit manual" (Kinney 1979: 149).

The first SAS dealing exclusively with analytical auditing was SAS 23, "Analytical Review Procedures," issued in 1978. This pronouncement was superseded by SAS 56, "Analytial Procedures," which was issued in 1988. SAS 56 requires auditors to use analytical auditing procedures both in planning audit engagements and in evaluating the results of audit testing. When using analytical procedures in audit planning an auditor would consider the guidance provided by SAS 53 "The Auditor's Responsibility to Detect and Report Errors and Irregularities," SAS 54 "Illegal Acts By Clients", and SAS 59 "The Auditor's Consideration of an Entity's Ability to Continue as a Going Concern." These standards require the auditor to adopt an active role with respect to these items. SAS 56 implies that auditors would ordinarily also use analytical auditing procedures as part of normal audit substantive testing, although it does not require this for all audits. Specific analytical auditing procedures are not discussed in this pronouncement except for the comment that they range from simple comparisons to the use of complex models.

SAS 56 places upon the auditor a responsibility to evaluate significant unexpected differences that occur during the use of analytical procedures. This requirement makes it prudent for auditors to carefully plan their analytical procedures so that they do not generate needless investigatory work.

Another concept discussed in SAS 56 is the relationship between high levels of assurance from analytical procedures and the predictability of the underlying relationship being examined. Relationships in a stable environment, involving income statement accounts, and nondiscretionary transactions are mentioned as providing greater predictability.

One aspect of detection risk that is related to analytical auditing is the quality of data used in an analytical auditing application. If the data on which an analytical auditing procedure is performed is of low quality (e.g., many errors or omissions) then the auditor might come to a wrong conclusion even though properly executing the analytical auditing procedure. Data errors may have led to inappropriate reliance on analytical procedures in one audit about which we have public information, "[the audit firm] ... relied extensively on an analytical test of the loss reserves to evaluate reserve adequacy. Although the methodology was basically sound, the results were inadequate because they were based on ... [the client] ... supplied data which contained numerous errors" (Securities and Exchange Commission 1978).

Auditors have a professional responsibility to insure that the data is reliable enough for the conclusion expressed. As noted in SAS 56, "In most instances, it would not be necessary to subject such data to audit testing: rather, the auditor would establish the reliability of the data by considering the source of the data and the conditions under which it was gathered (AICPA 1988: 6). The factors listed below affecting the reliability of data are summarized from SAS 56. It should be noted that the word "reliability" used in this context may be interpreted as relative strength of the data as an evidence source rather than as whether there are or are not errors or omissions in the data.

- External independent data sources are generally of higher reliability than internal data sources.
- Data is of higher reliability if sources within an entity which are responsible for the data production are independent of those parties on whom the data reports.
- Data produced from a reliable system of internal control is generally better than data from a poor system of internal control.
- Data subjected to some degree of testing, either current or prior year, is generally of higher reliability than data which has not been tested.
- Data from a variety of sources is generally more reliable than data from a single source, since inconsistencies may be more obvious.

SAS 36, "Review of Interim Financial Information," was issued in 1981. It discusses inquiry and analytical review procedures as the two procedures auditors should apply to interim financial information (e.g., quarterly data) in order to provide limited assurances with respect to such information. The analytical review procedures listed are virtually the same as the three procedures previously discussed in connection with the SSARS pronouncements.

INSTITUTE OF INTERNAL AUDITORS PROFESSIONAL STANDARDS

The Institute of Internal Auditors (IIA) is a professional association similar to the AICPA except that its interest is primarily internal auditing rather than public accounting. The IIA issued its first professional standards in 1978 when it issued *Standards for the Professional Practice of Internal Auditing*. This pronouncement consisted of a general set of standards governing the conduct of internal auditing. This general guidance was followed by a series of specific standards titled Statements on Internal

Auditing Standards (SIAS). The SIAS Numbers 1, 2, and 3, issued in 1985, reveal no specific guidance concerning analytical auditing.

U.S. FEDERAL GOVERNMENT

The U.S. federal government has not issued standards that apply to all types of auditors. Standards have been issued by various agencies or branches that apply to specific types of audits and/or auditors.

One set of guidance that applies to a significant number of auditors may be found in the pronouncements of the U.S. Securities and Exchange Commission (SEC). These pronouncements, however, are only binding on the audits of public companies and have very little in the way of specific audit guidance that is not contained in the previously discussed AICPA standards.

A fairly broad set of standards may be found in the *Standards for Audit of Governmental Organizations, Programs, Activities & Functions,* (1981 revision) which were originally issued in 1972 by the U.S. General Accounting Office (GAO). These have been known as the "yellow book" standards due to the color of its cover when originally issued. The GAO has also issued numerous other types of guidance such as *Federal Cognizant Agency Audit Guidelines* (1985) and *Compliance Supplement for Single Audits of State and Local Governments* (1985). Even more specific guidance may be found in specific audit requirements for various federal programs. The GAO guidance must be followed in audits of federal organizations, programs, activities, as well as funds received by organizations external to the federal government such as government contractors. Auditors planning federal organization or fund related audits should review applicable federal pronouncements to make sure they have identified all required procedures and disclosures. Any specific analytical audit requirements should be uncovered in such a review. The most cost-effective way to identify specific federal standards and requirements is usually through a subscription service which integrates and indexes this type of literature. Alternatively, an auditor may write directly to the U.S. Government Printing Office, Superintendent of Documents, Washington, D.C. 20402, to order copies of specific publications of interest.

DETERMINING A MATERIALITY LIMIT FOR ANALYTICAL AUDITING

SAS 47, "Audit Risk and Materiality in Conducting an Audit," re-emphasizes that auditors must make preliminary judgments (estimates) about overall materiality in order to appropriately plan an audit. It also states that the design of specific audit tests should reflect the auditors judgment about what could be material in that account or class-of-transactions. This means that auditors should have a specific materiality limit in mind when designing analytical auditing procedures. In other words, they should determine in advance what will be a significant difference between the actual result and projected result from the analytical auditing procedure. This standard also requires an auditor to determine likely (estimated) error in an account that has been tested and aggregate this likely error with several other classes of error in order to evaluate their impact on the overall financial statements. This means that if an analytical audit procedure indicates a difference between actual and projected results that exceeds what the auditor judges to be a normal difference (nonsignificant difference), the auditor must include this excess difference as a likely error, to be aggregated with other classes of error. The exception to this would be when the auditor obtains either a satisfactory explanation for the difference or appropriate assurance from other audit procedures that the likely error does not in fact exist.

A practical question that an auditor must answer is, "What is an appropriate materiality amount for conducting an analytical auditing test?" There are many different approaches to answering this question. One approach is to use a percentage of assets or revenues that varies according to the size of the company being audited. One widely used audit guide suggests the following sliding scale to determine overall engagement materiality:

Larger of Total Assets or Total Revenue is	Percentage
Below $100,000	4
Above $100,000 to $1,000,000	2
Above $1,000,000 to $3,000,000	1.5
Above $3,000,000 to $5,000,000	1
Above $5,000,000	0.7

Source: Carmichael, Meals, Huff and Anderson. 1986: pp. 2-12 and 2-13. Reprinted with permission.

The overall materiality level is then used to determine a materiality level for individual accounts. The account materiality is established as $1/3$ to $1/6$ of overall engagement materiality, depending on the auditor's risk assessment with respect to that account. For example, assume we are auditing a company with $750,000 in revenues and $300,000 in assets. We would compute an overall materiality limit for the entire audit of $15,000 ($750,000 times 2%). If we were planning an analytical auditing procedure for the Sales Salaries Expense account which has a balance of $40,000 and is judged to be a low risk account, an appropriate materiality limit (tolerable error) for that account according to the previous guide could be $5,000

($15,000 times ⅓). This means a difference would have to exceed $5,000 in order to be judged material. Let us further suppose that we apply time-series analysis to the account and judge a $3,000 difference between actual and projected results to be significant based on the nature of the procedure and the variability in the account. The size of our actual difference would then determine what additional work, if any, was needed. Three possible differences and the related audit conclusion are:

Difference Range	Conclusion
$0 to $2,999	Difference insignificant based on precision of test, no audit work beyond preliminary audit program necessary.
$3,000 to $4,999	No additional work required, but amount of difference in excess of $2,999 must be included in likely error analysis at conclusion of audit.
$5,000 or more	Additional audit testing of account necessary to explain difference exceeding $5,000.

What constitutes a significant difference for planning the test depends on the imprecision inherent in the analytical auditing procedure selected and the variability for the account. Some analytical auditing procedures are less powerful and therefore more imprecise in making projections. They will generally be expected to have larger significant differences. Likewise, some accounts have greater variability and may therefore be harder to model closely.

When the expected significant difference from an analytical auditing procedure exceeds the materiality limit for the account, the evidential value of the analytical auditing procedure is greatly reduced and may be negligible. If, in the previous example, the analytical auditing procedure of time-series analysis had resulted in the auditor using a significant difference of $7,000, then time-series analysis would not ordinarily have been selected as an analytical auditing technique for the account unless other audit procedures were planned for the account. The expected error from time-series analysis would have been too large for it, by itself, to provide adequate assurance about the account.

Once a significant difference is established, however, amounts less than that should be attributed to the general imprecision of the procedure, not to actual or likely errors in the account. Only differences exceeding the significant difference would be regarded as likely error.

AUDIT RISK

SAS 47, "Audit Risk and Materiality in Conducting an Audit," defines audit risk as "the risk that the auditor may unknowingly fail to appropriately modify his opinion on financial statements that are materially misstated." In other words, it is the chance that the auditor will give a report that everything is acceptable when there is really something materially wrong. SAS 47 requires an auditor to plan an audit to limit audit risk to an appropriately low level. Audit risk for the overall engagement would reflect the audit risk from all the individual areas of the audit. An auditor has to use professional judgment to aggregate the risk from the individual areas of the audit in order to determine overall audit risk.

When we consider audit risk at the account level, SAS 47 identifies three main components: inherent risk, control risk, and detection risk. The risk at the account level may be modeled using the formula

$$AR = I \times C \times D,$$

where:

AR is overall audit risk for the account.
I is inherent risk for the account. Inherent risk is the susceptibility of an account to error assuming there are no internal controls.
C is control risk. Control risk is the chance that the internal accounting control system will not prevent or detect material errors.
D is detection risk. Detection risk is the chance that an auditor's procedures will not detect material errors that have occurred. The two main classes of audit procedures used to detect errors are tests of details of balances and analytical auditing procedures.

Audit risk may be assessed in either quantitative or qualitative terms. If an auditor were able to quantify each of the previous factors then the formula could be used to calculate the exact amount of audit risk faced from the account. Most auditors do not attempt to do this, except for certain statistical sampling tests, but rather make a qualitative assessment of each of the factors in the formula. In a typical small business audit, for example, the assessment is usually as follows:

Inherent risk—High By default due to auditor not wanting to invest time to make an actual assessment.
Control risk—High Due to small number of personnel and limited controls typically found in small businesses.
Detection—Low Since the two previous items were assessed as "High" the detection risk must be "Low."

In order to achieve a "Low" detection risk, an auditor must select either several substantive audit procedures or a single substantive procedure for the account that will reduce the risk of not detecting a material error. If a single procedure is selected then it must have sufficient detection power to reduce the risk of nondetection to a low level. If two or more substantive procedures are selected, then they must jointly have sufficient detection power. For example, if we were auditing the Sales Salary Expense account, a regression model might provide enough detective power by itself and could be the only procedure we would apply to the account. On the other hand, if we simply compared Sales Salary Expense to the prior year amount, that might not have enough detective power by itself. Accordingly, we might combine that with a direct test of some of the transaction comprising the Sales Salary Expense balance.

Little guidance is found in the authoritative professional literature for auditors wanting to make a quantitative assessment of the detection risk from analytical review procedures. Probably one of the best comments is from the *Extent of Audit Testing* study "the effectiveness depends on the technique employed, the assurance with respect to the expected norms and the ability to obtain satisfactory explanations for significant fluctuations" (CICA 1980: 77). This study then goes on to provide the following guidance:

	Risk level attributable to analytical review
Low risk (very effective)	30%
Moderate risk (reasonably effective)	50%
High risk (somewhat effective)	70%

(CICA 1980: 99)

These percentages appear to be somewhat higher than similar non-authoritative guidance in the U.S. literature which generally seem to recommend a risk assessment of about 20% more in each of the three categories. The difference may be due to the fact that the applications envisioned in the U.S. literature may be traditional procedures which do not warrant a lower level of risk. The difference merely serves to illustrate the difficulty in making a valid quantitative assessment of audit risk components.

The previous discussion would be incomplete if we did not note that there are many other risk models in the audit literature in addition to the SAS 47 model previously discussed. These other models include different terms and formulas. Some of them are quite complex. However, the SAS 47 risk model is probably the most widely used risk model for financial auditing that can be directly related to analytical auditing.

EVALUATING GOING-CONCERN RISK VIA A DISCRIMINATE MODEL

As previously noted, in some circumstances auditors are required to assume an active role in assessing going-concern status. This means that they must be alert for or seek out possible indications of going-concern problems. One indicator of going-concern problems is adverse key financial ratios. Some researchers have identified certain key ratios and combined them into a single model through a statistical technique called discriminant analysis. These discriminant models can be used to produce a single score, called a "Z" score, which indicates if a problem exists. There are numerous different discriminant models in the research literature since different researchers have come up with slightly different ratios in their models. The interpretation of the Z score differs for each model.

One discrimant model that is fairly widely used was developed by Edward I. Altman for nonpublic companies. It incorporates five different financial ratios and is of the form

$$Z = .717 \ X_1 + .847 \ X_2 + 3.107 \ X_3 + .420 \ X_4 + .998 \ X_5,$$

where:

X_1 = Working Capital/Total Assets,
X_2 = Retained Earnings/Total Assets,
X_3 = Earnings Before Interest, Taxes/Total Assets,
X_4 = Book Value of Owners' Equity/Total Liabilities,
X_5 = Sales/Total Assets.

(Source: Altman, 1983: 121. Reprinted with permission.)

Using this model to determine if an individual company has a potential going concern problem is quite simple. An auditor simply calculates the five ratios indicated, substitutes them for their respective Xs in the equation, and sums the equation to produce a Z score for the company. The Z score thus produced may be interpreted by placing it in the appropriate area, based on its numeric value, in the line which follows:

Bankruptcy	No Clear	Bankruptcy
Highly	Signal	Highly
Likely	Given	Unlikely

```
                1.23                    2.90
                 |                       |
_____|_____|_____
                          .
```

For example, a Z score for a company of 3.65 would place it on the right side of the line in the area where bankruptcy is highly unlikely. This model had a 94 percent success rate in classifying a sample of 66 bankrupt and nonbankrupt companies. The average Z score for the bankrupt companies in the sample was .15 while the nonbankrupt companies had a Z score of 4.14. These mean values could also be marked on the preceding line. This model could, therefore, provide a strong early warning signal about going concern problems especially if a company's Z score was tracked over a period of years on a carry-forward schedule.

WORKING PAPER DOCUMENTATION OF ANALYTICAL AUDITING PROCEDURES

A review of SAS 41 "Working Papers" and other relevant SASs indicates that analytical auditing procedures applied as substantive tests should have the following audit working paper documentation:

- Audit risk analysis
- Analytical procedure description
- Analytical procedure computations
- Significant differences noted
- Follow-up and conclusions about significant differences
- Error aggregation schedule including significant differences indicating likely errors

The first and last items would normally be omitted if the analytical procedures were performed as part of the audit planning process. They would not be necessary because, in that case, the procedures would be focused on risk analysis and not error detection.

The risk analysis would normally take place in the audit planning memo or similar documentation. It should indicate that materiality and audit risk were appropriately considered when selecting specific analytical auditing procedures. The assertion or assertions toward which the analytical auditing is directed should also be indicated.

The specific analytical procedures to be performed should be clearly described in the audit program or similar documentation. The specific parameters for the test, such as what constitutes a significant difference, should be part of this description.

The working papers should contain either summary or detailed data about the analytical auditing calculations performed. If the data used in the calculations was financial in nature, then it should be clearly noted by the auditor that the data were appropriately taken from the client's accounting system. Also any verification procedures performed should be detailed. If the data is economic or operating data that did not come from the client's accounting system then the source and any verification procedures should be clearly noted. The working papers should clearly indicate significant differences noted from the analytical auditing procedures.

All work performed, if any, in investigating significant differences and conclusions reached about such differences should be clearly described in the working papers. Finally, it is important that the working papers provide a clear indication that any significant differences indicating likely or actual error either resulted in adjusting entries or were considered in an overall error aggregation schedule as required by SAS 47.

Working paper documentation of analytical procedure description, analytical procedure computations, significant differences noted, and follow-up/conclusions about significant differences are illustrated in Chapter 8 in conjunction with the illustration of a simple reasonableness test for payroll expense.

REFERENCES

American Institute of Certified Public Accountants. "The Auditor's Responsibility to Detect and Report Errors and Irregularities" *Statement on Auditing Standards Number 53.* New York: AICPA, 1988.

American Institute of Certified Public Accountants. "Illegal Acts by Clients" *Statement on Auditing Standards Number 54.* New York: AICPA, 1988.

American Institute of Certified Public Accountants. "Analytical Procedures" *Statement on Auditing Standards Number 56.* New York: AICPA, 1988.

American Institute of Certified Public Accountants. "The Auditor's Consideration of an Entity's Ability to Continue as a Going Concern" *Statement on Auditing Standards Number 59.* New York: AICPA, 1988.

American Institute of Certified Public Accountants, AICPA *Professional Standards,* Volumes 1 and 2. New York: AICPA, 1987.

Altman, E. I. *Corporate Financial Distress—A Complete Guide to Predicting, Avoiding, and Dealing with Bankruptcy.* New York: John Wiley & Sons, 1983.

Canadian Institute of Chartered Accountants. *Extent of Audit Testing.* Toronto: Canadian Institute of Chartered Accountants, 1980.

Carmichael, D. R., D. R. Meals, B. N. Huff and J. Anderson. *Guide to Audits of Small Business*—Volume 1. Fort Worth, Texas: Practitioners Publishing Company, 1986.

Institute of Internal Auditors. *Standards for the Professional Practice of Internal Auditing.* Altamonte Springs, Florida, 1978.

International Auditing Practices Committee. "International Auditing Guidelines," in AICPA *Professional Standards,* Volume 2, 12,001–12,590. New York: AICPA, 1987.

Kinney, W. R., Jr. "The Predictive Power of Limited Information in Preliminary Analytical Review: An Empirical Study," *Journal of Accounting Research* (Vol. 17 Supplement 1979): 148–165.

Kinney, W. R., and G. L. Salamon. "The Effect of Measurement Error on Regression Results in Analytical Review," *Symposium on Auditing Research III* by an Audit Group at the University of Illinois at Urbana-Champaign, 1979: 49-64.

U.S. General Accounting Office. *Compliance Supplement for Single Audits of State and Local Governments,* revised edition. Washington, D.C.: Superintendent of Documents, U.S. Government Printing Office, 1985.

U.S. General Accounting Office. *Federal Cognizant Agency Audit Organization*

Guidelines. Washington, D.C.: Superintendent of Documents, U.S. Government Printing Office, 1985.

U.S. General Accounting Office. *Standards for Audit of Governmental Operations, Programs, Activities and Functions,* revised edition. Washington, D.C.: Superintendent of Documents, U.S. Government Printing Office, 1981.

U.S. Securities and Exchange Commission. "Accounting Series Release Number 241." February 10, 1978.

4
Simple Trend Analysis

Trends are systematic changes or patterns occurring through time. Trend analysis is concerned with identifying these systematic patterns to be used in predicting the future from past data. Basically this involves identifying past patterns, constructing a model based on the past patterns and using this model to predict the current value for the item of audit interest. Thus, when an auditor can identify trends or patterns in past data, he or she can use them to predict what the current book values should be.

Since all auditors use simple trend analysis techniques at some point in time, it is necessary for all auditors to have a basic understanding of time-series trend concepts. This chapter first discusses basic time-series concepts. It then explains and illustrates the most common trend analysis techniques employed by auditors. This knowledge will enable auditors to better plan and execute various types of simple techniques and to appreciate the more complex techniques. All types of trend analysis techniques, even the simple ones employed daily by auditors, are a type of modeling. As with all types of modeling, the model's assumptions are critical to its success. Therefore, we will also briefly discuss the basic assumptions of each different model presented.

CAUSAL VERSUS NONCAUSAL MODELING

There are many different factors that potentially could cause trends. If we attempt to analyze data and identify factors that we think could *cause* changes in the data we are performing Causal Analysis or Causal Modeling. If we simply try to construct a model using past relationships between variables without regard as to whether one variable actually causes another variable to change then we are using Noncausal Modeling. Either approach is acceptable as long as the auditor knows the strengths and weaknesses of both the modeling approach and the individual variables being employed.

One of the simplest ways of describing a trend is as a function of time. For example, an auditor may use a carry-forward schedule to plot sales for the last five years. The auditor then uses the average change over the last five years to predict what a reasonable amount for current year sales is. This is usually Noncausal Modeling because basic economic theory makes it doubtful that time is the factor causing the change in sales for most firms. It is more likely that other economic variables are causing sales to change. Many variables, such as sales, may change at a relatively constant rate through time thus allowing us to use the time rate of change to predict what level they will be at in the future but this does not mean that time causes them to change. Describing a trend as a function of time is frequently called time-series modeling.

A more complex way of describing a trend is as a function of several different variables that might cause the trend. For example, an auditor may determine that sales are related to four different variables, the level of advertising expenditures, interest rates, prior industry sales, and foreign currency exchange rates. If the auditor can construct a mathematical model based on the relationship between sales and the four variables then the auditor can use this model to predict current period sales. This is called Causal Modeling or structural modeling because it is presumed that the variables used to predict the sales, either directly caused the changes in sales or were surrogates for factors that caused the changes.

In this book we will discuss and explain both causal and noncausal modeling approaches. This chapter discusses the following simple types of time-series modeling which are noncausal modeling approaches:

- Current period to prior period change method.
- Simple trend statements.
- Graphical method.
- Average change method.
- Weighted average method.
- Weighted moving average method.

These methods can all be efficiently and effectively employed in a normal audit setting with only a pencil, paper, and pocket calculator. Of course, as with most types of recurring audit schedules or computations, a micro-computer based electronic spreadsheet package, such as Lotus 1-2-3™, can make them even more efficient.

CURRENT PERIOD TO PRIOR PERIOD CHANGE METHOD

The current period to prior period change method of analytical auditing is probably the most frequently used analytical procedure. A recent national survey of CPAs indicated that 88.5% of the auditors surveyed indicated that they *always* used this procedure in audits. That was the highest percentage of all the techniques included in the survey (Daroca and Holder 1985: 85).

Most auditors set their working papers up in a format that facilitates this type of analysis. They put current year book balances and prior year audited balances in adjacent columns, making comparison of the two figures relatively easy. It is more difficult to decide what kind of comparison to make between the two figures—dollar change, percentage change, or both dollars and percentage change? The author recommends the latter method since the auditor is typically concerned with both large dollar fluctuations, because of the possibility of a material misstatement, and large percentage fluctuations, because they might signal a larger problem even if they are not themselves material from a dollar standpoint.

The current period to prior change method appears to implicitly assume that the prior period amount is being projected into the current period. This is only true if the auditor determines what will be a material difference without giving consideration to the direction of probable change from the prior period. If the auditor assumes that the prior period will change by a certain dollar or percentage amount and determines the material difference based on this assumed change plus an amount for random error, then the auditor is in effect projecting a change from the prior period through the process of determining the material difference.

A practical problem that auditors must deal with in using this method is deciding what will be a significant difference. It is recommended that the criteria for a significant difference be determined before the technique is applied in order to avoid biased decisions. When a significant difference is defined in terms of dollars it should be related to the materiality level for the engagement. The exact relationship to materiality will depend on when during the audit the technique is applied. For example, if the technique is applied during the planning stages of the audit a higher limit might be used since the auditor might only want very large fluctuations signaled by the technique. If applied as a substantive auditing procedure a lower limit may be used since the analytical auditing technique may be the only audit technique applied to certain accounts. As indicated in the preceding chapter, a significant difference of from ⅓ to ⅙ of engagement materiality is frequently used.

It is also difficult to specify an appropriate percentage difference. Experience suggests that in many situations perhaps a different percentage should be used for balance sheet accounts and income statement accounts due to the normally larger fluctuations in some balance sheet accounts. Ten percent appears to be a common percentage to use on the balance sheet accounts. The difference used on the income statement accounts should be related to the expected change in revenues. If the auditor knows that revenues were expected to increase by 15% in the current year then it would be foolish to use a 5% difference in the income statement accounts as being significant since most of the income statement accounts would probably be flagged for further work by the 5% limit. The limit set by the auditor should be comprised of the expected change in the revenue account plus an additional amount (say 5%) for normal random fluctuations in the numbers. So, if a 15% increase in revenues were projected then a reasonable limit might be 20% for the income statement accounts. This assumes that most of the expenses will be directly variable in nature and not semivariable or fixed expenses.

When an auditor uses a dual-screen test, such as both dollar and percentage change, another question is how to structure the dual-screen. Should it be both dollar *and* percentage change or *either* dollar *or* percentage change? It would appear that the *either/or* combination would be most appropriate for normal audit substantive tests. This type of dual-screen in a substantive audit test is illustrated in Figure 4.1, Current period to prior period change method working paper.

SIMPLE TREND STATEMENTS

A popular variation on the Current Period To Prior Period Change Method is to construct Simple Trend Statements which include several prior years data as in the following example:

	1984	1985	1986	1987	1988
Sales	$12,345	$15,699	$17,111	$18,645	$19,190

These statements can improve an auditor's analysis by including not only the prior year but several prior years' data. This provides the auditor with a better perspective in case the immediate prior year was not appropriately representative.

This type of analysis can also be performed in a common- size format where each subsequent year is expressed as a percentage of a base year which is usually the earliest year presented. The previous sales amounts would appear as the following percentages:

	1984	1985	1986	1987	1988
Sales	100.0	127.2	138.6	151.0	155.4

ABC CORPORATION
WORKING TRIAL BALANCE
DECEMBER 31, 1988

'T.E.M.
1-7-88

WTB 1

ACCOUNT TITLE	WKPP REF	PER AUDIT 12-31-87	PER BOOKS 12-31-88	AJE #'S	ADJUSTMENTS DEBITS	ADJUSTMENTS CREDITS	RJE #'S	RECLASSIFICATIONS DEBITS	RECLASSIFICATIONS CREDITS	ADJUSTED BALANCE 12-31-88	% CHG PRIOR YEAR	$CHG PRIOR YEAR	> 10% CHG AND > $10,000 CHG COMP.PRIOR YR.
BALANCE SHEET													
CASH	A	15244.45	17628.57							17628.57	0.16	2384.12	.
MARKETABLE SECURITIES	B	244567.00	400000.00							400000.00	0.64	155433.00	++++++++++
ACCOUNTS RECEIVABLE	C	215895.65	238474.32				1	15000.00		253474.32	0.17	37578.67	++++++++++
INVENTORIES	D	196219.98	265840.98	1		24000.00				241840.98	0.23	45621.00	++++++++++
PREPAID EXPENSES	E	29104.21	32375.80							32375.80	0.11	3271.59	.
OTHER CURRENT ASSETS	F	22662.50	39262.76							39262.76	0.73	16600.26	++++++++++
TOTAL CURRENT ASSETS		723693.79	993582.43							984582.43	0.36	260888.64	++++++++++
PLANT AND EQUIPMENT	G	1433461.48	2028169.04							2028169.04	0.41	594707.56	++++++++++
OTHER ASSETS	H	38727.77	45319.22							45319.22	0.17	.6591.45	.
TOTAL ASSETS		2195883.04	3067070.69							3058070.69	0.39	862187.65	++++++++++
NOTES PAYABLE TO BANKS	AA	16992.45	44900.00							44900.00	1.64	27907.55	++++++++++
CURR PORTION OF LT DEBT	BB	350000.00	325678.33							325678.33	-0.07	-24321.67	.
ACCOUNTS PAYABLE	CC	72772.55	92036.88				1		15000.00	107036.88	0.47	34264.33	++++++++++
ACCRUED LIABILITIES	DD	99552.76	159319.39							159319.39	0.60	59766.63	++++++++++
INCOME TAXES PAYABLE	EE	43771.11	25198.11							25198.11	-0.42	-18573.00	.
TOTAL CURRENT LIABILITIES		583088.87	647132.71							662132.71	0.14	79043.84	++++++++++
LONG-TERM LOANS	FF	1176572.59	1913261.37							1913261.37	0.63	736688.78	++++++++++

(*continued*)

Figure 4.1 Current period to prior period change method working paper.

ABC CORPORATION
WORKING TRIAL BALANCE
DECEMBER 31, 1988

T.E.M.
1-7-88

W-B 1

ACCOUNT TITLE	WKPP REF	PER AUDIT 12-31-87	PER BOOKS 12-31-88	AJE #'S	ADJUSTMENTS DEBITS	ADJUSTMENTS CREDITS	RJE #'S	RECLASSIFICATIONS DEBITS	RECLASSIFICATIONS CREDITS	ADJUSTED BALANCE 12-31-88	% CHG PRIOR YEAR	$CHG PRIOR YEAR	> 10% CHG AND > $10,000 CHG COMP.PRIOR YR.
DEFERRED INCOME TAXES	GG	55667.00	17894.00							17894.00	-0.68	-37773.00	.
COMMON STOCK	HH	16500.00	18500.00							18500.00	0.12	2000.00	.
ADDIT PAID-IN-CAPITAL	II	91422.00	99422.00							99422.00	0.09	8000.00	.
RET EARNINGS EXCL NI	JJ	234876.44	152240.38							152240.38	-0.35	-82636.06	.
CURRENT YEAR NET INCOME		37756.14	218620.23		24000.00	0.00				194620.23	4.15	156864.09	++++++++++
TOT LIAB & SHARE EQUITY		2195883.04	3067070.69		24000.00	24000.00		15000.00	15000.00	3058070.69	0.39	862187.65	++++++++++
OUT OF BALANCE BY		0.00	0.00		0.00	0.00		0.00	0.00	0.00			

INCOME STATEMENT
****

ACCOUNT TITLE	WKPP REF	PER AUDIT 12-31-87	PER BOOKS 12-31-88	AJE #'S	ADJUSTMENTS DEBITS	ADJUSTMENTS CREDITS	RJE #'S	RECLASSIFICATIONS DEBITS	RECLASSIFICATIONS CREDITS	ADJUSTED BALANCE 12-31-88	% CHG PRIOR YEAR	$CHG PRIOR YEAR	> 10% CHG AND > $10,000 CHG COMP.PRIOR YR.
NET SALES	PL-1	1134252.99	1641914.21							1641914.21	0.45	507661.22	++++++++++
COST OF SALES	PL-10	682685.71	857725.04	1	24000.00					881725.04	0.29	199039.33	++++++++++
GROSS PROFIT		451567.28	784189.17							760189.17	0.68	308621.89	++++++++++
SELLING EXPENSES	PL-20	323495.61	479957.75							479957.75	0.48	156062.14	++++++++++
ADMINISTRATIVE EXP	PL-30	12042.84	12037.21							12037.21	-0.00	-5.63	.
INTEREST EXPENSE	PL-40	51394.31	45744.02							45744.02	-0.11	-5650.29	.
OTHER EXPENSE	PL-50	1706.45	2483.00							2483.00	0.46	776.55	.
INCOME BEFORE INC TAX		62928.07	244367.19							220367.19	2.50	157439.12	++++++++++
PROVISION FOR INCOME TAX	PL-60	25171.93	25746.96							25746.96	0.02	575.03	.
NET INCOME		37756.14	218620.23		24000.00	0.00				194620.23	4.15	156864.09	++++++++++

SELECTED RATIOS:

LIQUIDITY**

CURRENT RATIO	1.24	1.54	1.49
QUICK RATIO	0.82	1.01	1.01
SALES / WORKING CAP.	8.07	4.74	5.09
CASH FLOW / CURR. MAT. L.T.D. (ASSUMES DEPRECIATION IS 10% OF FIXED ASSETS)	0.52	1.29	1.22

PROFITABILITY**

GROSS PROFIT %	0.40	0.48	0.46
NET PROFITS / SALES	0.03	0.13	0.12
NET PROFITS / ASSETS	0.02	0.07	0.06
NET PROFITS / OWNERS' EQUITY	0.10	0.45	0.42

EFFICIENCY RATIOS************************************

INVENTORY TURNOVER (COST OF GOODS SOLD / AVG. INV.)	3.48	3.71	4.03
ACCOUNTS RECEIVABLE TURNOVER (NET CREDIT SALES / AVG. ACCTS. REC.)	5.25	7.23	7.00
SALES / ASSETS	0.52	0.54	0.54

CAPITAL STRUCTURE RATIOS************************

DEBT / OWNERS' EQUITY	4.77	5.27	5.58
EARN. B. INT., TAX. / INTEREST	2.22	6.34	5.82
FIXED ASSETS / OWNERS' EQUITY	3.77	4.15	4.36

Figure 4.1. (*Continued*).

63

The common-size format has the advantage of more clearly revealing the relative year to year change.

GRAPHICAL METHOD

Another common analytical auditing method involves constructing a graph of past values to use in projecting a current period value. This method is really an extension of the previous method. It is relatively simple when applied in its basic form. The auditor uses graph paper and plots the past data values thereby constructing a "scatter graph" or "scatter diagram". The auditor then visually inspects the scatter diagram to see if any trend or pattern is apparent. If a trend is apparent the auditor then draws in a freehand (visually fitted) line that best depicts the trend through the data values. When the fitted line is extended to the current period it provides a projected value for the current period.

Normally the line fitted by the auditor would be a straight line; however, the auditor could fit other types of lines. A curve of some type may be appropriate if the relationship appears nonlinear. Fitting a curve, though, requires a higher level of skill than fitting a straight line. One way around this problem is for the auditor to employ a data transformation to change the data trend from a nonlinear to linear relationship. A data transformation is simply a mathematical function that changes the relative magnitude of the data. Common data transformations are:

- Cube   raise a number to the third power.
- Square   raise a number to the second power.
- Square Root   raise a number to the ½ power.
- Logarithm   convert a number to its base 10 logarithm or to its natural logarithm.
- Reciprocal   divide 1 by a number.

We will illustrate the effects of a data transformation by using a logarithm (base 10) to convert a nonlinear sales growth rate:

Year	Sales	Yearly Change in Sales	Logarithm of Sales	Change in Logarithm
1	$10,000		4.000	
2	20,000	$10,000	4.301	.301
3	40,000	20,000	4.602	.301
4	80,000	40,000	4.903	.301

Although we have not graphed the previous sales data, it should be clear from an inspection of the data that sales were doubling each year, clearly not a linear trend. The sales line would be a sharply increasing curve. On the other hand, the logarithms of the sales amounts are increasing at a constant annual amount, a linear trend. An auditor could therefore first plot the sales amounts on graph paper, visually inspect them to determine that they appeared to be nonlinear, convert the sales amounts to their logarithms, and then plot the logarithms on graph paper. If the logarithms appear linear, the auditor could then fit a line to the logarithms and use that line to project a sales amount expressed as a logarithm. The projected sales expressed as a logarithm can then be converted to a dollar sales amount by taking its antilog. The computation of the logarithm, antilogs, or other transformations can be done in a few seconds on many pocket calculators.

Scatter graphs are beneficial even if the author does not want to draw in a line to fit the data. They facilitate visual examination of the data for trends or patterns. This added information can aid the auditor in choosing the most appropriate model from the several modeling techniques that are presented later in this chapter. It may also be appropriate to employ data transformations in these modeling techniques.

The most difficult part of the graphical method is deciding what will constitute a significant difference from the projected value. The book value for the current period may be close to the projected value but the critical question is how close does it have to be to say that the book figure is reasonable? One approach is to measure the difference on the graph paper and evaluate it in terms of materiality or tolerable error for the account. If the difference is appropriately less than materiality or tolerable error then it can be said that the graphical method projection supports the book figure.

Another approach to determining whether a significant difference exists between the projection and the book amount is to draw upper and lower boundary lines around the fitted line. These lines should be equidistant from the fitted line and be far enough away to include all of the plotted data points except those judged to be "outliers" (abnormal or nontypical values). If the book value falls within the upper or lower boundary line then the auditor accepts the book figure as being supported by the graphical projection method.

We can illustrate this method by assuming the following sales data and then plotting the sales data as illustrated in Figure 4.2, Scatter diagram of sales data:

Year	Sales	Year	Sales
1978	$100,000	1983	$184,000
1979	124,000	1984	221,000
1980	128,000	1985	287,000
1981	147,000	1986	271,000
1982	177,000	1987	310,000

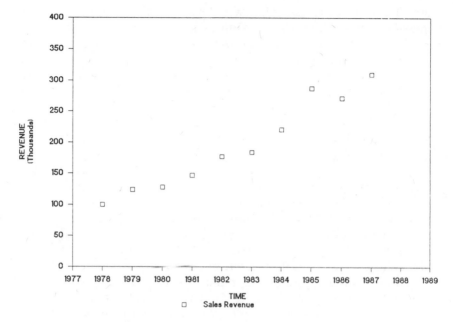

Figure 4.2. Scatter graph of sales data.

Before plotting the sales data we must decide which variable to place on the horizontal axis and which variable to place on the vertical axis. This is a fairly easy decision. In time-series analysis, time is normally placed on the horizontal axis and the variable of interest, sales in this case, is placed on the vertical axis. A tougher decision is deciding how to scale the graph. The scale on the horizontal axis should be in single units of time, years in our example. The scale on the vertical axis will be in units of the variable being plotted there, dollars normally. The key question though is how many dollars should each unit on the graph represent as different scales will make the trends on the graph appear quite different. One approach to dealing with this problem is to always scale the data in terms of either the materiality level for the engagement or some financial statement constant such as 10% of revenues. The auditor who uses one of these two scales consistently with different clients will then get graphs that behave in the same fashion. The auditor will then be in a better position to relate the experience from one client to another in making judgments about the behavior of graphs. In our example, we scaled the graph in $50,000 increments.

Once we have plotted the data, the next step is to draw in a line that best fits the data points. The easiest way to accomplish this is to lay a clear plastic ruler with its edge through what appears to be the middle of the data points. Then adjust the ruler up or down so that an approximately equal number of observations lie on each side of the ruler. Figure 4.3, Scatter graph with fitted line, illustrates how a fitted line might appear.

If, while fitting a line, an individual data point appears to be significantly out of the range of the other data points then it may be an abnormal value, called an "outlier." Outliers can be ignored in fitting the line if the conditions causing them are not expected to reoccur. The auditor should try to determine what unusual conditions caused the value to be abnormal and whether those conditions might have been repeated in the year being audited.

Once the line has been fitted in, the next step is to use it to make a projection for the year being audited. In our example, let us assume we wish to make a sales projection for the year 1988 that we can compare to recorded book sales using our materiality limit for 1988 to judge whether there is a significant difference. We can do this by locating the point representing 1988 on the horizontal axis, drawing a vertical line up from this point until it intercepts the projection line, and then drawing a horizontal line to the left from the point of interception. The point where this last line intercepts the vertical axis would be our estimated value for the sales in 1988. Using Figure 4.3, this estimate would be approximately $327,000 from our previous example.

If we draw in upper and lower boundary lines we do not have to go

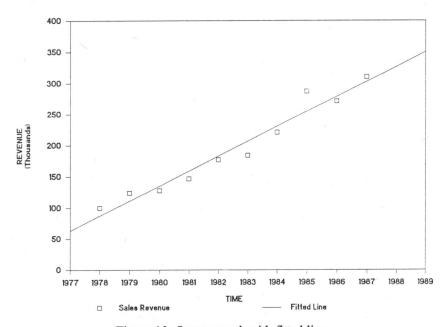

Figure 4.3. Scatter graph with fitted line.

through the previous steps to determine whether the analytical auditing procedure supports the recorded book figure. We can simply plot the data point representing 1988 book sales and see if it falls between the upper and lower boundary lines. If it does, then we can conclude the analytical auditing procedure supports the book figure. If it does not fall between the boundary lines the amount of difference between the book figure and the nearest boundary line will tell us how significant the problem is. This approach is illustrated in Figure 4.4, Scattergraph with boundary lines. In Figure 4.4, 1988 sales are assumed to be $370,000. The boundary lines are drawn $30,000 above and below the fitted line. The boundary lines have been extended to include the farthest point away from the fitted line during the base period. This point was the 1985 sales amount that falls right on the upper boundary line. Figure 4.4 clearly reveals that the 1988 sales amount falls outside the boundary lines. We therefore conclude that 1988 sales of $370,000 are not supported by the graphical method with a $30,000 boundary line.

The major limitation of the graphical method is that the boundary lines can be fairly far from the fitted line unless the data pattern is very regular. This difference should be evaluated in terms of materiality or tolerable

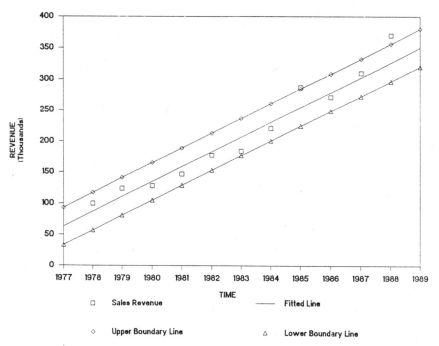

Figure 4.4. Scatter graph with boundary lines.

error for the account to determine how good the model is. If the individual boundary lines are farther from the projection line than 50% of tolerable error for the account, then the model would be considered to have weak evidential value. It is important to remember that an auditor can always construct a model by drawing in a line but the resulting model may not have much evidential value if the fitted line does not reflect a reasonably tight underlying pattern or relationship.

AVERAGE CHANGE METHOD

The average change method is based on the assumption that the average change in the past two or more periods can be applied to the most recent prior period to predict the current period value. The average change can be measured in terms of either the average dollar change or the average rate of change.

We will illustrate the computation of the average dollar change method first by using the sales data from our previous example. The formula for this method is:

Average Dollar Change = (Dollar Value for Most Recent Period

— Dollar Value For Earliest Period)/

(Number of Data Periods − 1).

When this formula is applied to the sales data we get:

Average Dollar Change = ($310,000 − 100,000)/(10 − 1)

Average Dollar Change = $23,333

The average dollar change is then added to the sales for the most recent period to get the projection for the next period, the period under audit:

1987 Sales + Average Dollar Change = 1988 Sales Projection

$310,000   + $23,333   = $333,333

The average rate change method is very similar and involves computing the average rate of change over the base period and then applying that rate to the most recent years sales to project a sales amount for the current period. A simplified formula for this is:

Average rate of change = (Most Recent Year's Sales / Earliest Year's

Sales) − 1 / (Number of Year's Data − 1).

When we apply this formula to the illustrative data we get the following:

Average rate of change = ($310,000 / $100,000) − 1 / (10 − 1)

Average rate of change = .23

The average rate of change is then multiplied by the sales for the most recent period to get the amount of projected increase for the next period:

1987 Sales + (1987 Sales × Average Rate of Change) = 1988 Sales

$310,000 + ($310,000 × .23) = $371,300

The simplified formulation of the rate of change model presented here gave a significantly higher prediction than the amount of change model. This will always happen when a trend is increasing since the rate of change is applied to the most recent period which is the highest period when a trend is increasing. Therefore, the rate of change model should only be used when the annual dollar change in the variable appears to be increasing and is not approximately the same from period to period. This model involves some very simplistic assumptions. More accurate projections are possible using more complex models such as present-value models.

WEIGHTED AVERAGE CHANGE METHOD

The average change method previously presented gives an equal weight to each prior period. That is, all prior periods are averaged in equally. If an auditor believes that some prior periods are more representative than others, the auditor may want to weight the prior periods in some unequal manner. There are many ways to do this but one common way is to weight the individual year's change in the reverse order of their age similar to the computation in sum-of-the-year's digits depreciation. This method could be applied to either the annual dollar change model or the annual rate of change model, although the author believes it is more appropriate for the former since the latter automatically gives a higher estimate. The application of this technique in terms of annual dollar change is illustrated in the following computation using the same data in the previous example:

Year	Age	Amount	Annual Change	Weight	Change × Weight
1978		$100,000	(none since this is is the earliest year)		
1979	1	124,000	$24,000	1/45	$ 530
1980	2	128,000	4,000	2/45	180

Year	Age	Amount	Annual Change	Weight	Change × Weight
1981	3	147,000	19,000	3/45	1,270
1982	4	177,000	30,000	4/45	2,670
1983	5	184,000	7,000	5/45	780
1984	6	221,000	37,000	6/45	4,930
1985	7	287,000	66,000	7/45	10,260
1986	8	271,000	−16,000	8/45	−2,740
1987	9	310,000	39,000	9/45	7,800
Sum	45				$25,580

The weighted average dollar change of $25,580 calculated in this computation is then added to the prior period amount to make a projection for the current period:

1987 Sales + Average Dollar Change = 1988 Sales Projection

$310,000 + $25,580 = $335,580

WEIGHTED MOVING AVERAGE METHOD

The weighted moving average methods are also techniques for giving more weight to the most recent periods. The rationale is simply that the auditor believes the most recent periods might be more typical than less recent periods. We will only look at one weighted moving average method, exponential smoothing. This method is most effective with time-series that have no strong trend or seasonal patterns. It is, therefore, not appropriate for the same data set that we have used in our previous illustrations although we will use that same data set so a comparison can be made with the predictions from the other techniques.

To use the exponential smoothing model the auditor has to decide how much weight is to be given to the most recent data observation. The next most recent period's forecast, not data observation, is then weighted with the complement (1 − weight) of the weight chosen for the most recent data observation and the two values are summed to produce next year's forecast. This method can also be applied to either the dollar change model or the rate of change model. The formula is:

Next Year's Forecast = (Current Year's Data Value × Weight)

+ (Prior Year's Forecast × Weight)

If we assume that the most recent data observation is to receive a 70 percent weight and apply this formula in terms of dollar change to our previous data set we get the following results:

(A) Year	(B) Actual Sales	(C) .70 × Sales	(D) .30 × Prior Forecast	(C + D) Current Forecast for Next Year
1978	$100,000			$100,000*
1979	124,000	.70 × $124,000	.30 × $100,000	116,800
1980	128,000	.70 × 128,000	.30 × 116,800	124,640
1981	147,000	.70 × 147,000	.30 × 124,640	140,292
1982	177,000	.70 × 177,000	.30 × 140,292	167,988
1983	184,000	.70 × 184,000	.30 × 167,988	179,196
1985	221,000	.70 × 221,000	.30 × 179,196	208,459
1986	287,000	.70 × 287,000	.30 × 208,459	263,438
1987	310,000	.70 × 310,000	.30 × 263,438	296,031

*Assume actual sales are forecasted sales to start the model.

Since the exponential smoothing model is simply a type of weighted moving average, as with most moving averages, its projections will always lag an increasing trend. The 1988 sales prediction of $296,031 is, therefore, significantly less than the predictions obtained from the other models with the same data set.

COMPARISON OF THE MODELS PREVIOUSLY PRESENTED

In order to help auditors to decide which of the methods presented in this chapter may be most appropriate for them, we conclude this chapter with a brief summary of the previous models along with their major strengths and weaknesses. Please remember that each of the time-series models presented is a simple noncausal model. Noncausal time-series models present an extra risk since past trends may change abruptly if the underlying causal factors vary significantly.

Current Period To Prior Period Change Method

This model compares the current period amount to the prior period amount and evaluates the difference for reasonableness.

Strengths   Easy to compute. Computations easily fit normal working paper format.

Weaknesses   Sometimes difficult to prespecify what differences will be significant. Ignores information in prior periods which are earlier than the most recent prior period.

Simple Trend Statements

This method compares the current period to several prior periods and evaluates the difference for reasonableness.

Strengths   Easy to prepare working paper in a carry-forward schedule format.

Weaknesses Sometimes difficult to prespecify what differences will be significant.

Graphical Method

This method involves plotting several periods data values on graph paper so the auditor can visually fit a line to the data and make a projection.

Strengths   Relationships may stand out more clearly in a graphical form.

Weakness   It may be difficult to fit a line to nonlinear data. It can be difficult to determine whether the projected value is close enough to support the book value.

Average Change Method

This method involves computing either the average dollar change or average rate of change over several data periods and using this to make a projection.

Strengths   Easy to compute. Can provide a good projection.

Weaknesses All prior periods are averaged even though some may be more significant than others.

Weighted Average Method

This method involves the weighting of prior periods in accordance with their perceived significance and then calculating a weighted average change.

Strengths   Auditor can assign heavier weights to periods perceived to be of more importance.

Weaknesses   Computations can be difficult when done manually. It is often difficult for an auditor to know what weighting scheme is best without time consuming experimentation.

Weighted Moving Average

This method involves computing a moving average where the most recent period can receive a heavier weight than the earlier periods.

Strengths   Computations are relatively simple. Provides good projections when trend is stable.
Weaknesses   It is difficult for an auditor to know what weighting scheme is best other than by time consuming experimentation. Models projections always lag a changing trend.

REFERENCES

Blocher, E., and J. J. Willingham. *Analytical Review—A Guide to Evaluating Financial Statements.* New York: McGraw Hill Book Company, 1985.
Daroca, F. P., and W. W. Holder. "The Use of Analytical Procedures in Review and Audit Engagements," *Auditing: A Journal of Practice & Theory* (Spring 1985): 80-92.
May, G. S., L. H. Beard, and J. P. Bedingfield. "Regression Analysis In Smaller Audits," *The CPA Journal* (November 1976): 78-80.
Willis, R. E. *A Guide to Forecasting for Planners and Managers.* New Jersey: Prentice-Hall, Inc., 1987.

5
Basic Ratio Analysis

The simple trend analysis discussed in the previous chapter had one possibly overall significant limitation—it focused solely on a single account and therefore reflected only the information inherent in that single account. Ratio analysis overcomes this limitation because it can capture the information content from two different accounts or areas. "The use of ratios exploits the fact that account balances may be correlated due to both the double-entry nature of accounting and multiple accounting effects of systematic management decision strategies" (Arrington, Hillison, and Icerman 1983: 158). This chapter will explore the basics of ratio analysis as applied in analytical auditing.

Ratio analysis in its basic form consists of a comparison of two or more variables. Its attempts to reduce these variables to a relationship which is simpler and more understandable. In performing ratio analysis, auditors should establish ratios which are meaningful because of the underlying economic relationships they express and their easy comparability to other entities.

ADVANTAGES OF RATIO ANALYSIS

A recent national survey of auditors indicated that over 50% of auditors *always* employ some type of ratio analysis with the computation of the current ratio, gross margin on sales, and profit margin on sales being the more common ratios (Daroca and Holder 1985:85). What accounts for this popularity as an analytical auditing technique? An analysis of the advantages of ratio analysis provides an answer to this question.

Most auditors presume, based on their training in economic theory, that certain internal relationships exist between accounts. One significant advantage of ratio analysis is that it can capture in a single measure these internal relationships or underlying economic conditions even though they may be relatively complex. For example, the current ratio can represent the economic condition of short-term liquidity even though it might take a fairly complex model to describe how short-term liquidity in a firm changes. A ratio then, can be a surrogate or substitute, for an underlying economic condition. The ratio can utilize the fact that different account balances may be correlated (related to each other) and that there may be effects in several different accounts from a single transaction due to the nature of double-entry accounting.

Another advantage of ratio analysis is that it converts from dollars (absolute amounts) to ratios (relative amounts) thereby facilitating comparisons between different size firms and in different time periods. For example, if Company A has six times the revenues of Company B it is difficult to compare in a meaningful way Company A's gross profit of $45,657,231 with Company B's gross profit of $6,789,432. Yet we can compare fairly readily Company A's gross profit ratio of .45 to Company B's gross profit of .43. Likewise, if Company Y has experienced a sixfold increase in revenue over the last seven years it would be difficult to make meaningful dollar comparison of gross profits in year one with year seven. We can, however, make a meaningful analysis of the gross profit ratio over the same time period.

It is important for the auditor using ratio analysis to remember that research indicates disaggregated data is more effective for this type of test than aggregated data. This means that auditors should use monthly balances or balances by segment or product line rather than overall data for the year. The research further indicated that even *material* error may not show up in ratio analysis performed on aggregated data (Kinney 1987: 59-73).

TYPE OF ANALYSIS

The major benefit of ratio analysis is that it establishes relationships among variables that can be compared to a norm or projected result. By making that comparison an auditor can determine whether a firm's ratio is approximately the same as the norm or whether a significant difference exists. Norms for ratio analysis are usually established in one of three ways—theoretical norms, time-series analysis or cross-sectional analysis. A theoretical norm is one established based on economic theory. Unfortunately, we do not have many widely accepted theoretical models to provide us with normative ratios. We will explore the meaning of the last two sources of norms in order to better understand the types of comparisons we can make.

A frequently neglected aspect of ratio analysis is that the variability (fluctuation) of a ratio can be as important as its mean (average) value. The variability of a ratio tells an auditor both how much fluctuation in a ratio is normal and whether the ratio is suitable for comparison to other ratios. For example, suppose the current ratio for a client and the client's industry were:

	1984	1985	1986	1987	1988
Client	2.2	2.7	1.9	1.8	2.3
Industry	2.3	2.4	2.0	2.1	2.3

As indicated below the mean (average) value for the client and industry are reasonably close (client is within 2% of industry) indicating that the two ratios can be compared. However, the variability (fluctuation) as indicated by the standard deviation is significantly different (client is 225% of industry) for the client and industry. This indicates that perhaps the mean values should not be directly compared.

	Mean	Standard Deviation
Client	2.18	.36
Industry	2.22	.16

Although there are other measures of variability, the standard deviation is a common statistical term that is easy to understand. One standard deviation is the distance from the mean value that includes approximately two-thirds of the data points in a normally distributed data series. An auditor would normally be reluctant to make a direct comparison of client and industry ratio means if the variability of the client ratio was more than one standard deviation larger or smaller than the variability of the industry ratio. If the variability of the ratios is large then some type of indirect comparison of client and industry might be more appropriate. The standard deviation is also easy to use since it can be readily computed in a few seconds by a single function key on many inexpensive pocket calculators.

TIME-SERIES ANALYSIS OF RATIOS

Time-series analysis is the examination of the behavior of a variable through time to detect patterns or trends which may be useful for making projections. In the previous chapter we discussed it as a means of analyzing the behavior of a single account and explained several techniques for making such an analysis. All of the techniques for analyzing a single account may also be applied to financial ratios. Thus we can use the same techniques to establish an historical pattern for a ratio and then use that pattern to make a decision as to whether the same ratio is significantly different in the period under audit. Therefore, time-series analysis can enable us to establish a norm for a ratio by examining its behavior over time.

We will illustrate the application of time-series analysis to ratio analysis by an example. Suppose we are auditing ABC Company in year 6 and have computed the inventory turnover ratio for the prior five years as being:

Year	Inventory Turnover Ratio
1	4
2	4.6
3	4.4
4	4.3
5	4.3

The year 6 inventory turnover has been calculated to be 4.9 and we need to determine whether that is a reasonable figure. One approach would be to use the graphical approach discussed in the previous chapter to construct a scatter graph for the past five years and fit in a line to the past values. We could then draw in two boundary lines around the fitted line to determine an interval of acceptable values. These boundary lines would determine whether the current year turnover of 4.9 is reasonable. As can be seen in Figure 5.1, Turnover ratio scatter graph, the current year turnover of 4.9 is outside the boundary lines and therefore unreasonable. The auditor would have to search for the reason which could range from a simple change in inventory management policies to an inaccurate physical inventory or inventory cutoff problems.

CROSS-SECTIONAL ANALYSIS OF RATIOS

Cross-sectional analysis is the examination of the behavior of a variable among different entities at a single point in time. In effect, a norm for the variable is established by reference to the group behavior. As applied to ratio analysis, this means that we can establish a norm by reference to industry data. The ratio of an individual firm can then be compared to the industry norm to see if there is a significant difference.

Time-series and cross-sectional analysis are combined when we analyze the behavior of an individual firm *and* the related industry through

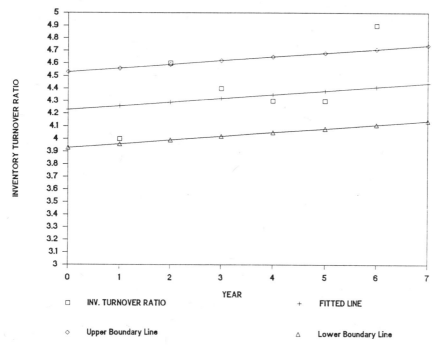

Figure 5.1. Turnover ratio scatter graph.

time. Auditors accomplish this by plotting both firm and industry ratios on carry-forward schedules which are updated yearly. This type of analysis provides much more information than separate application of the two techniques.

COMMON RATIO CLASSIFICATION

A typical set of financial statements provides the opportunity to compute, literally, thousands of ratios. A key question for the average auditor is therefore, what ratios should I compute? There is, of course, no universally accepted answer to this question. Experience indicates, however, that minimum audit coverage should include computation of an appropriate ratio in at least seven different categories. This will provide the auditor with data about most of the significant underlying economic relationships for the normal firm. Individual industry differences will usually call for some industry specific ratios in addition to this minimum list:

Category	Example Ratio
• Short-term liquidity	current ratio
• Cash position	cash/total assets
• Inventory turnover	inventory/sales
• Receivables turnover	quick assets/sales
• Return on investment— (Profitability)	net income/total assets
• Financial leverage	total liabilities/net worth
• Capital turnover	cash flow/total assets

Each of the preceding seven categories represents a factor that is an underlying economic dimension of an individual firm. Within each category there are many possible ratios to compute. Research suggests that the ratios within each category are normally highly correlated (tend to move together). This means that it is normally only necessary to compute one appropriate ratio in each category. The auditor's task, therefore, becomes one of selecting an appropriate ratio in each of the categories.

KEY SHORT-TERM LIQUIDITY RATIOS

Short-term liquidity indicates the ability of a firm to meet its short-term liabilities solely from the existing current financial resources of the company. One basic assumption behind this measure is that the firm will continue operating normally with no additional borrowing taking place or no unusual asset liquidations. This means that we are really measuring the ability of the firm to meet its obligations based on its condition at a single point in time.

A good short-term liquidity position indicates that a firm has effective receivables, inventory, and payables management. If analysis in either the receivables or inventory areas indicates a possible problem there, the auditor should be alert to the possibility of either a payables cutoff or recording problem which would give the appearance of good short-term liquidity. A poor short-term liquidity position may put unusual pressure on management thereby increasing risk of either unduly optimistic accounting estimates by management or an irregularity.

The four best ratios to measure the short-term liquidity for the normal firm are:

Ratio	Formula
Current ratio	current assets/current liabilities
Quick ratio	cash + cash equivalents + net receivables/current liabilities

Ratio	Formula
Current debt to assets ratio	current liabilities/total assets
Accounts payable turnover	365 days/{[(cost of goods sold − beginning inventory) + ending inventory]/average accounts payable}

Since these ratios basically measure the same underlying phenomena there is no real reason to prefer one over the other except possibly for the availability of comparative industry ratios. They should all indicate somewhat the same condition.

KEY CASH POSITION RATIOS

Cash position refers to the ability of a firm to retain an adequate amount of cash for normal operating purposes. The cash position reflects cash management.

A good cash position indicates that a firm has sufficient cash available to meet normal operating needs. An excess amount of cash may indicate potential problems if it is not earning an appropriate return and being accumulated for a specific purpose. Ideally there will be an arrangement with the firm's banks to earn interest on all cash deposits. Auditors should be alert to the possibility of cutoff errors in recording end of period interbank cash transfers that may improve a firm's cash position. A poor or negative cash position indicates that the firm's cash management policies may need reviewing. It can also mean a problem exists with respect to product profitability. Care should be taken to consider available lines of credit when analyzing the cash position since these can be almost immediate sources of cash if needed. When evaluating a poor cash position, auditors must consider the possibility that a company recorded payment of expenses but held back the physical mailing of the checks. Two ratios which measure cash position are:

Ratio	Formula
Cash to sales	cash or cash equivalent/sales
Cash to assets	cash or cash equivalent/total assets

KEY INVENTORY TURNOVER RATIOS

Inventory turnover refers to how many times in a particular period a firm sold its average inventory. A high inventory turnover indicates that a firm very quickly sells the equivalent of its average inventory. This ratio, in other words, reflects inventory management. This ratio is obviously more important to firms which have a higher percentage of assets tied up in inventories.

A high inventory turnover ratio could indicate that a firm has understated cost of goods sold through some type of error or that ending inventory is abnormally low for some reason. A low inventory turnover ratio may indicate that a firm has excess, obsolete, or slow moving inventory. It may also indicate possible errors in taking physical inventories or in recording adjustments based on physical inventories. Two inventory turnover ratios are:

Ratio	Formula
Inventory turnover	cost of goods sold/average inventory
Days sales in inventory	365 days/(cost of goods sold/average inventory)

KEY RECEIVABLES TURNOVER RATIOS

Receivables turnover indicates the number of times a year the average accounts receivable are converted to cash. It reflects, therefore, the effectiveness of accounts receivable management.

A high receivables turnover could indicate improved receivables management, a possible cutoff problem (i.e., sales recorded but invoices not yet mailed, unauthorized write-offs of bad debts) or improper use of credit memos. A low receivables turnover indicates possible problems with the collectibility of accounts receivable, billing procedures, or credit terms. Two common accounts receivable turnover ratios are:

Ratio	Formula
Accounts receivable turnover	credit sales/average accounts receivable
Accounts receivable collection period	365 days/(credit sales/average accounts receivable)

The use of credit sales is preferred in computing these ratios but if that figure is not readily available total sales may be employed instead. Of course, if a high percentage of sales are on a credit basis there will be only a minor difference between using credit sales or total assets.

KEY RETURN ON INVESTMENT (PROFITABILITY) RATIOS

Return on investment indicates the funds generated from operations in relation to the assets employed in operations. It reflects management's long-run success in selecting appropriate capital investment projects for the firm.

A good return on investment indicates that the firm has good earning power and is effectively using all its resources. Auditors should be alert to possible revenue or expense cutoff problems when return on investment is higher than expected. A poor return on investment indicates poor earning power in relation to assets employed in operations. Auditors should be alert for obsolete equipment that is not used in operations but still carried on the books. A poor return on investment may also be indicative of cutoff problems.

A detailed analysis of the components of revenue and expense is usually performed by an auditor as part of the comparison to prior years analysis (discussed in the previous chapter) or as part of the common-size statement analysis (to be explained in the next chapter). Common return on investment ratios are:

Ratio	Formula
Funds flow on assets	cash flow from operations/total assets
Net profit margin	net income after tax/net sales
Return on equity	net profit/common stockholder's equity

KEY FINANCIAL LEVERAGE RATIOS

Financial leverage indicates the degree to which the owner's investment has been leveraged with debt. In other words, the amount of debt financing in relation to stock investment in the company. The higher the degree of leverage the greater the potential profits to the owner if the business does well and the greater risk of bankruptcy if the business does poorly.

An unusually high financial leverage condition could indicate possible problems in recorded liabilities. It could also indicate that key debt covenant restrictions might be violated. A low financial leverage condition could indicate a possible unrecorded liability problem. Three key ratios which indicate financial leverage are:

Ratio	Formula
Liabilities to assets	total liabilities/total assets
Debt to equity	total liabilities/stockholders's equity
Debt payment coverage	cash flow from operations/current maturities of long-term debt

KEY CAPITAL TURNOVER RATIOS

Capital turnover is somewhat similar to return on investment but represents the flow of capital in operations rather than the return from operations. An abnormal capital turnover ratio can indicate a problem with recorded revenue or recorded assets. Three capital turnover ratios are:

Ratio	Formula
Liquid assets	current assets/total assets
Sales to assets	sales/total assets
Net worth to sales	owners' equity/sales

BEYOND THE BASIC SEVEN RATIO CATEGORIES

In addition to computing a ratio in the seven basic categories previously discussed, there are a number of other ratios that an auditor may want to compute either because they provide some type of specific information necessary to plan the audit or because they may constitute an audit test. Although many of these ratios are industry specific, the following list contains some which are of general interest:

Ratio	Audit Significance
Accounts receivable/number of credit customers	Measures average customer balance which may be significant in planning confirmations.
Bad debt allowance/accounts receivable	Auditor would expect this to remain relatively constant unless there has been a change in credit policy or collection effectiveness.
Gross profit/sales	Profitability measure that should be stable unless there has been a change in product cost or pricing.

Ratio	Audit Significance
Sales/units sold	The average sales price should be compared to company data on official sales prices and product mix to determine the degree of testing needed in the sales area.
Cash sales/sales	The cash mix of sales would normally be fairly constant from year to year, can indicate problem with credit sales if this is unusual.
Freight expense/units shipped	Indicates freight charge per unit and should be compared to freight rates for reasonableness.
Interest income/notes receivable	Should be close to stated interest rates.
Selling expenses/units sold	Indicates efficiency of sales effort and should be relatively stable unless sales activities have changed significantly.
Warranty expenses/units sold	Should be stable unless change in policy. Could indicate quality control problems, change in sales mix, change in customer mix.
Employee benefit expense/total payroll expense	Indicates cost of benefits on per person basis. Should be stable unless change in benefit package.
Total payroll expense/365	This computes the average daily payroll which should be stable except for change in wage rates or employee mix.
Payroll tax/total payroll expense	Measure of tax rate which should be close to statutory rates.

RATIOS SIGNIFICANT TO NONAUDITORS

In addition to ratios which provide information about specific factors which may affect the nature, extent, and timing of audit procedures, the prudent auditor may want to analyze some addition ratios simply because various financial statement users will be interested in them. It would be foolish in this age of litigation to ignore an item that an important statement user might attach significance to. Financial statement users which an auditor may be concerned about include stockholders, creditors, unions, and financial analysts.

An analysis of the annual reports of *Fortune* 500 companies found the following significant ratio appearance frequencies in the annual reports:

Ratio	Frequency
Earnings per share	100%
Dividends per share	98%
Book value per share	84%
Working capital	81%
Return on equity	62%
Profit margin	58%
Effective tax rate	50%
Current ratio	47%
Debt/capital	23%
Debt/equity	19%

(Gibson 1982: 20)

Shifting from annual reports to commercial loan departments, we find a slightly different picture. Commercial loan departments focus more on debt and liquidity ratios. One study found that commercial loan departments viewed, in descending order of importance, the (1) debt/equity ratio, (2) current ratio, (3) cash flow/current maturities of long-term debt ratio, and (4) fixed charge coverage ratio as the most important ratios (Gibson and Frishkoff: 436). Many of these same ratios commonly appear in loan agreements containing restrictions related to them.

PERFORMING RATIO ANALYSIS VIA AN EXPERT SYSTEM

Most auditors are aware of the possible automation of ratio computations by using electronic spreadsheet software such as Lotus 1-2-3™ and a microcomputer. This type of automation, though, only automates the computations, the auditor still has to apply considerable thought and expertise in interpreting the significance of the ratios computed. A new type of software called expert system software has recently arrived on the audit scene. This type of software offers the promise of automating much of the though process associated with certain analytical auditing applications.

Current expert systems in the auditing area are software packages that have stored the knowledge of an expert auditor in a particular aspect of auditing and can, therefore, aid a nonexpert auditor in making some of

TABLE 5.1. Sample Expert System Observations.

```
--------------------------------------------------------------------
!REPORT DATE:  11/30/85      TREND OBSERVATIONS AND COMMENTS      PAGE 1!
!PREPARED BY:                    BLUE WATER SAILBOATS                  !
!REVIEWED BY:                    DECEMBER 31, 1985                     !
!-------------------------------------------------------------------- !
!              ACCOUNTS RECEIVABLE/SALES--TREND DECISIONS              !
!              ========================================               !
!Based on the materiality limits specified, the following trends and/or!
!relationships were noted as possibly significant.  You should review and!
!evaluate the applicability of each observation and comment.          !
!                                                                     !
!   OBSERVATIONS              COMMENTS                                 !
!                                                                     !
!1. ALLOWANCE FOR BAD DEBTS   Are A/R writeoffs and the allowance   12!
!   INCREASED WHILE # OF DAYS account being accounted for consistently!
!   SALES IN RECEIVABLES      from year to year?                      !
!   DECREASED                                                         !
!                             Has the allowance account been reviewed 36!
!                             relative to the current receivables accounts?!
!                             Could the allowance account be excessive,!
!                             given current and historical collections?!
!                                                                     !
!                             Review subsequent collections on accounts 38!
!                             previously written off to assure that they!
!                             have been properly recorded.            !
!                                                                     !
!2. A/R TURNOVER              This could represent positive or improved 5!
!   INCREASED                 receivables management.                 !
!                                                                     !
!                             This could represent possible cutoff problems 7!
!                             (i.e. sales recorded but invoices not yet!
!                             mailed).                                !
!                                                                     !
!                             This could reflect improper use of credit 8!
!                             memos or unauthorized write-offs.       !
--------------------------------------------------------------------
```

Source: Financial Audit Systems. ANSWERS™ Users Guide. Raleigh, North Carolina: Financial Audit Systems) 1987: 110.31. Reprinted with permission.

the decisions in that area. The software should enable nonexpert auditors to improve the quality and consistency of their decisions in the audit area where the package provides assistance. They are not currently sufficiently "expert" to completely replace the human auditor in any area. It is unlikely that they will become this advanced within the next decade.

Different expert systems can utilize different reasoning schemes and different user interfaces. In order to explain this technology we will briefly discuss a commercially available expert system package for analytical auditing called ANSWERS™.

When using ANSWERS™ expert system software to perform ratio analysis you must first install the software on your microcomputer. Installation involves identification of the type of equipment you are using as well as making some choices about mode of operation. The next step is to input data for a particular client. Typically, input data would include the most recent five years of balance sheet and income statement data as well as desired materiality levels. The latter item would permit the software to decide what were significant deviations. The software would be instructed as to which ratios, from a large set of ratios, were desired to be calculated. The software would then calculate the specified ratios, identify significant trends or relationships noted in the ratios, and provide a list of interpretive comments about the trends noted. An example trend report with comments is provided in Table 5.1, Sample Expert System Observations. This type of software offers the promise of further automating the analytical auditing process.

Another application of expert system software to auditing is a situation where the expert system is continuously auditing the transaction flow in a large computer system. Transactions which are deemed to be unusual are selected for further investigation. Analytical auditing techniques comprise one mechanism used by this type of expert system to select unusual transactions. This type of software has already been implemented in some large computer systems (Vasarhelyi, Halper, and Pauly, 1988).

REFERENCES

Arrington, C. E., W. Hillison, and R. C. Icerman. "Research in Analytical Review: The State of the Art," *Journal of Accounting Literature* (1983): 151–185.

Blocher, E., and J. J. Willingham. *Analytical Review—A Guide to Evaluating Financial Statements.* New York: McGraw-Hill Book Company, 1985.

Chen, K. H., and T. A. Shimerda. "An Empirical Analysis of Useful Financial Ratios," *Financial Management* (Spring 1981): 51–60.

Cleverly, W. O., and K. Nilsen. "Assessing Financial Position with 29 Key Ratios," *Hospital Financial Management* (January 1980): 30–36.

Deakin, E. B. "Distributions of Financial Accounting Ratios: Some Empirical Evidence," *The Accounting Review* (January 1976): 90–96.

Daroca, F. P., and W. W. Holder. "The Use of Analytical Procedures in Review and Audit Engagements," *Auditing: A Journal of Practice & Theory* (Spring 1985): 80–92.

Financial Audit Systems. *ANSWERS—The Financial Expert System* (Version 2.5). Raleigh, North Carolina, 1987.

Gibson, C. H., and P. Frishkoff. *Financial Statement Analysis.* Boston: Kent Publishing Company, 1983.

Gibson, C. "Financial Ratios in Annual Reports," *The CPA Journal* (September 1982): 18–29.

Holder, W. W. "Analytical Review Procedures in Planning the Audit: An Application Study," *Auditing: A Journal of Practice & Theory* (Spring 1983): 100–107.

Imhoff, E. A., Jr. "Analytical Review of Income Elements," *Journal of Accounting, Auditing & Finance* (Summer 1981): 333–351.

Kennedy, H. A. "A Behavioral Study of the Usefulness of Four Financial Ratios," *Journal of Accounting Research* (Spring 1975): 97–116.

Kinney, W. R., Jr. "Attention-Directing Analytical Review Using Accounting Ratios: A Case Study," *Auditing: A Journal of Practice & Theory* (Spring 1987): 59–73.

McKee, T. E. *Analytical Techniques for Audit or Review Purposes* (CPE Coursebook). New York: AICPA, 1987.

Touche Ross. *Financial Analysis as an Audit Tool.* New York: Touche Ross & Co., 1981.

Vasarhelyi, M. A., F. B. Halper, and R. J. Pauly. "The Continuous Audit of Online Systems" AT&T proprietary document, 1988.

Whittington, G. "Some Basic Properties of Accounting Ratios," *Journal of Business Finance and Accounting* (Fall 1980): 219–232.

6

Common-size Statements and Microcomputer Applications

The previous chapter discussed the type of ratio analysis, known as financial ratio analysis, that is based on the computation of the relationship between varying financial statement accounts. This chapter explains a second type of ratio analysis called common-size statement analysis. This type of ratio analysis consists of reporting each item on the income statement or balance sheet as a percentage. In the case of the income statement, each item is reported as a percentage of total revenues. In the case of the balance sheet, each item is reported as a percentage of total assets. This means that all elements in both statements are displayed as percentages.

Although we will be discussing common-size statement analysis in terms of converting a complete statement to common-size percentages, many auditors use the common-size method to compute selected individual ratios without converting the entire statement. Thus, they use some common-size elements but not necessarily a complete common-size statement. Some examples of ratios frequently computed in this manner are:

- gross profit/sales
- cost of goods sold/sales
- bad debt expense/sales
- commission expense/sales
- sales discounts/sales
- selling expense/sales
- warranty expense/sales
- net income/sales

- working capital/total assets
- total liabilities/total assets

HOW COMMON-SIZE STATEMENTS CAN BE BENEFICIAL

Since common-size statements are a type of ratio analysis they have the same two major benefits as financial ratio analysis. The first benefit is that dollars (absolute amounts) are converted to percentage (relative amounts) thus making comparisons to other firms of a larger or smaller size easier and much more meaningful. This approach also facilitates comparisons to the same firm in different time periods when the firm has experienced substantial growth or significant inflation. The second benefit is that many of the common-size percentages (ratios) have intrinsic meaning because they reflect underlying economic relationships. The previous list provides some prime examples of common-size ratios, reflecting underlying economic relationships, that are typically computed by auditors even in the absence of complete common-size statements. For example, consider the ratio—commission expense/sales. If the commission compensation plan is such that commissions are only paid based on sales made, we know that sales cause commissions to be incurred by the firm. Thus, this ratio reflects the underlying economic cause-effect relationship.

Another advantage of common-size statements is that they facilitate an analysis of the relative structure or size of the entity. This is primarily useful in audit planning since it makes the probable audit approach much more readily apparent. Audit planning is assisted due to the fact that one aspect of materiality depends on the relative magnitude of an item. Thus, auditors normally assess some aspects of audit risk based on the relative size of an account and allocate resources accordingly. For example, assume we are planning an audit and construct a common-size balance sheet to assist us in the audit planning process. If we note an inventory figure of 62%, we immediately know that inventory will require a high percentage of audit resources since it is such a significant component of assets. Conversely, if we note an inventory figure of 8% we know that the audit effort allocated to inventory will be rather small because the account is not very material, at least in a quantitative sense. The norm used in this type of analysis would be the average or typical audit. This could be the typical audit for all types of industries or it could be the typical audit in a particular industry. The comparison base would depend on the background and experience of the auditor using the common- size analysis in the audit planning process.

For a second example of the use of common-size analysis in the audit planning process, let us assume that we look at a common-size income statement and note six different expense accounts that are each less than

3% of sales. We would immediately know, based on quantitative materiality aspects, that these expense accounts probably would not require direct tests since they are individually immaterial. Our audit approach in this case might be to obtain audit assurance from both compliance tests of the cash disbursements system and from analytical auditing procedures (procedures in addition to the common-size analysis), performing no direct tests of the expense account balances. The exception to this approach would be if any of the expense accounts are of a type, such as legal expense, where we would want to breakdown the balance for other purposes, such as a liability search. Because of this ability to facilitate size analysis of financial statement accounts, one of the primary uses of common-size statements is in planning an audit.

FORMATS FOR COMMON-SIZE STATEMENTS

There are two basic formats for common-size statement analysis. Both formats stem from the need to establish a norm against which to compare the current period percentage and to determine if there is a significant difference. The first format involves using a time-series set of common-size statements. A common approach is to use the five years immediately prior to the year being audited. This approach involves establishing a norm from these five prior year statements via one of the five time-series analysis tools discussed in Chapter 4. The second format involves using a cross-sectional set of time- series statements. This means that the auditor uses one or more sets of other financial statements in the same time period to assist in evaluating the current period statements being audited. This approach involves establishing a norm either via analysis of several competitors in the same time period or by use of an industry average. When competitor's statements are used, the competitors, in effect, become an industry average against which to compare the company being audited.

Table 6.1, Common-size Statements—Time-series Analysis, illustrates the first format via a five-year series of time-series statements. The relationships in the five prior year statements have been projected into the current period via the average change method in order to establish a norm. A difference of more than 20% in the balance sheet or 10% in the income statement from the current year amount has been defined as a significant difference and flagged for audit attention. If this approach were used in planning an audit, the auditor would consider what changes from the prior year audit plan would be necessary to cope with the significant differences noted. For example, if plant and equipment were down by more than 20% the auditor might want to increase the amount of assurance that equipment retirements were properly recorded. He or she

TABLE 6.1. Common-size Statements—Time-series Analysis.

	1984	1985	1986	1987	1988	AVERAGE $ CHANGE PROJECTION FOR 1989	ACTUAL 1989	% DIFF	? INDICATES SIGNIFICANT DIFFERENCE
ASSETS:									
Cash & Equivalents	7.9	8.9	9.4	8.5	9.1	9.4	9.7	0.03	.
Trade Receivables	29.1	27.4	28.7	28.6	30.4	30.7	27.5	-0.11	.
Inventory	27.9	26.5	26.7	27.3	25.6	25.1	22.3	-0.11	.
Other Current Assets	2.2	2.3	2.6	2.3	4.5	5.7	6.0	0.06	.
Total Current Assets	67.1	65.1	67.4	66.7	69.6	70.2	65.5	-0.07	.
Plant and Equipment	25.4	27.9	26.2	26.2	27.4	27.9	30.2	0.08	.
Intangibles	0.8	0.9	0.6	0.8	2.2	3.2	3.4	0.08	.
Other Non-current Assets	6.7	6.1	5.8	6.3	0.8	0.6	0.9	0.44	?
Total	100.0	100.0	100.0	100.0	100.0		100.0		
LIABILITIES AND EQUITY:									
Current Notes Payable	13.3	12.3	13.4	13.1	10.2	9.6	11.2	0.17	.
Trade Payables	14.0	13.6	14.7	14.1	14.4	14.5	11.1	-0.23	?
Income Taxes Payable	2.1	4.5	2.6	2.8	3.4	3.9	4.1	0.04	.
Other Current Liabilities	12.3	11.9	12.2	12.2	15.0	15.8	13.1	-0.17	.
Total Current Liabilities	41.7	40.3	42.9	41.7	43.0	43.3	39.5	-0.09	.
Long-term Debt	14.6	16.7	13.4	14.8	18.0	19.0	17.9	-0.06	.
Deferred Taxes	3.6	0.0	4.5	2.9	5.5	6.2	9.7	0.56	?
Other Non-current Liab.	2.4	3.3	2.7	2.7	2.2	2.2	2.9	0.35	?
Stockholders' Equity	37.7	39.7	36.5	37.9	31.3	30.0	30.0	0.00	.
Total	100.0	100.0	100.0	100.0	100.0		100.0		
REVENUES:									
Sales	82.3	88.0	89.0	83.1	80.2	79.7	87.6	0.10	.
Interest Income	4.4	0.3	0.1	2.2	6.5	7.3	2.3	-0.68	?
Miscellaneous Revenues	13.3	11.7	10.9	14.7	13.3	13.3	10.1	-0.24	?
Total	100.0	100.0	100.0	100.0	100.0		100.0		
EXPENSES:									
Cost of Goods Sold	45.9	46.9	46.4	46.3	44.9	44.7	43.5	-0.03	.
Selling, Gen. & Admin. Exp.	36.7	37.4	37.8	37.2	34.7	34.2	32.4	-0.05	.
Interest Expense	1.2	4.5	6.5	3.4	3.3	4.7	6.9	0.45	?
Miscellaneous Expenses	1.5	3.1	6.5	3.2	2.1	2.3	3.4	0.47	?
Income Tax Expense	6.9	5.1	1.3	5.1	6.9	6.9	9.7	0.41	?
Total	92.2	97.0	98.5	95.0	91.9		95.9		
NET INCOME	7.8	3.0	1.5	5.0	8.1		4.1		

DIFFERENCES FLAGGED: ? SIGNS INDICATE DIFFERENCES EXCEEDING 20% ON THE BALANCE SHEET AND 10% ON THE INCOME STATEMENT

might accomplish this either by reliance on client internal controls over the process or by increased direct tests.

Table 6.2, Common-size Statements—Cross-sectional Approach, contains comparisons of XYZ Company's common-size statements with the common-size statements of three competitors (competitors A, B, and C) of similar size. A weighted average has been computed from the competitors' statement percentages to form a norm against which to compare XYZ Company. However, the weights applied to the statements were not equal. Competitor A was judged by the auditor to be more directly comparable to the client being audited so the auditor gave those statements double the weight of the other two competitors. The weights employed were:

TABLE 6.2. Common-size Statements—Cross-sectional Approach.

	COMPETITOR A	COMPETITOR B	COMPETITOR C	WEIGHTED AVERAGE OF COMPETITORS	XYZ COMPANY	PERCENTAGE DIFFERENCE	INDICATES SIGNIFICANT DIFFERENCES
ASSETS:							
Cash & Equivalents	7.9	8.9	9.4	8.5	7.8	0.09	.
Trade Receivables	29.1	27.4	28.7	28.6	30.4	-0.06	.
Inventory	27.9	26.5	26.7	27.3	25.6	0.06	.
Other Current Assets	2.2	2.3	2.6	2.3	4.5	-0.94	?
Total Current Assets	67.1	65.1	67.4	66.7	68.3	-0.02	.
Plant and Equipment	25.4	27.9	26.2	26.2	28.7	-0.09	.
Intangibles	0.8	0.9	0.6	0.8	2.2	-1.84	?
Other Non-current Assets	6.7	6.1	5.8	6.3	0.8	0.87	?
Total	100.0	100.0	100.0	100.0	100.0		
LIABILITIES AND EQUITY:							
Current Notes Payable	13.3	12.3	13.4	13.1	10.2	0.22	?
Trade Payables	14.0	13.6	14.7	14.1	14.4	-0.02	.
Income Taxes Payable	2.1	4.5	2.6	2.8	3.4	-0.20	.
Other Current Liabilities	12.3	11.9	12.2	12.2	15.0	-0.23	?
Total Current Liabilities	41.7	40.3	42.9	41.7	43.0	-0.03	.
Long-term Debt	14.6	16.7	13.4	14.8	18.0	-0.21	?
Deferred Taxes	3.6	0.0	4.5	2.9	5.5	-0.88	?
Other Non-current Liab.	2.4	3.3	2.7	2.7	2.2	0.19	.
Stockholders' Equity	37.7	39.7	36.5	37.9	31.3	0.17	.
Total	100.0	100.0	100.0	100.0	100.0		
REVENUES:							
Sales	92.3	98.0	99.1	95.4	90.2	-0.05	.
Interest Income	4.4	0.3	0.0	2.3	6.5	1.86	?
Miscellaneous Revenues	3.3	1.7	0.9	2.3	3.3	0.43	?
Total	100.0	100.0	100.0	100.0	100.0		
EXPENSES:							
Cost of Goods Sold	55.9	56.9	56.4	56.3	54.9	0.02	.
Selling, Gen. & Admin. Exp.	26.7	27.4	27.8	27.2	24.7	0.09	.
Interest Expense	1.2	4.5	6.5	3.4	3.3	0.01	.
Miscellaneous Expenses	1.5	3.1	6.5	3.2	2.1	0.33	?
Income Tax Expense	6.9	5.1	1.3	5.1	6.9	-0.37	?
Total	92.2	97.0	98.5	95.0	91.9		
NET INCOME	7.8	3.0	1.5	5.0	8.1		

DIFFERENCES FLAGGED: ? MARKS INDICATE DIFFERENCES EXCEEDING 20% ON THE BALANCE SHEET AND 10% ON THE INCOME STATEMENT

Competitor A	50%
Competitor B	25%
Competitor C	25%

A difference of 20% in the balance sheet and 10% in the income statement between XYZ Company's current year percentage and the weighted average of the competitors (the norm) was defined by the auditor as being significant.

USING ELECTRONIC WORKSHEET SOFTWARE TO PREPARE
COMMON-SIZE STATEMENTS

Large main-frame electronic computers did not have a widespread significant impact as audit tools because they were not cost-effective for many audit tasks. Consequently, their principal use in auditing was either to run some specialized time-sharing programs such as earnings per share computation programs or to run generalized audit software packages that enabled auditors to extract and manipulate data in computer files. Neither of these applications impacted to a great degree on the average audit practitioner since they were specialized applications that were not directly applicable to day-to-day audit activities.

Widespread change began to occur in the early 1980's due to the widespread proliferation of both microcomputers and a type of microcomputer based software called "electronic worksheet software." These tools began to dramatically change the shape of auditing practice. The change they started is accelerating and it appears that audits in the next decade will be much more highly automated than in the past. The tools offer auditors ways of performing many audit tasks with a tremendous increase in efficiency. They also offer the potential for increased audit effectiveness by providing a cost-effective practical way for auditor's to perform certain advanced and very powerful analytical auditing procedures, such as regression analysis, that previously were not widely used. They have spawned a range of new software tools for auditors to use that expands almost daily.

Microcomputers and related software facilitate the automation of analytical auditing in the following manner:

- Easy storage and retrieval of models. A model created for one year can now be easily used the following year.
- Sensitivity or "what if" analysis can be easily performed thus encouraging auditors to ask more questions and experiment with alternative solutions.
- Design of models to accommodate a specific client situation.
- "Integrated software" offers a variety of programs such as word processing, electronic worksheet, and database programs in a single package that can work together on a single task without cumbersome file transfers or recopying of data.
- Computerized decision support systems can almost automatically select the appropriate model and test to see if its assumptions are reasonably met.
- Programs can simplify the interpretation of analytical model test

results by providing audit conclusions in an easily understandable narrative form rather than in statistical terms.

(Kunitake, Luzi, and Glezen 1985: 24-25)

Of course, new technology usually takes a considerable time to be absorbed by a profession due to change inhibitors such as the need for capital investment, training, quality control, and research as to effectiveness in widely varying conditions. Nevertheless, it is quite clear that auditors who are going to remain efficient in today's increasingly competitive environment will have to embrace the audit automation advantages offered by microcomputers and electronic worksheet software. This section explains the basic features of this type of software and shows how it can be used to prepare common-size statements.

Electronic worksheet software offers a number of advantages in preparing common-size statements. First, it can greatly speed up the computations. For example, a column of 80 different numbers can be added in less than a second. Second, the computations are much more accurate. Computers very rarely have hardware failures that would cause a mistake. Third, the software can be instructed to flag significant deviations, thus performing an attention directing role. Fourth, when a standard template (a set of software instructions) is created it normally can be used for a great many different clients with only minor modifications. Finally, if a firm develops a standard template it can be easily copied thus making it available to all members of the firm. This may facilitate quality control if the software has been appropriately developed with the diverse needs of different auditors in mind.

Electronic worksheet software is microcomputer software that can perform the same types of activities an auditor could do manually with a pencil and a worksheet with a large number of columns and rows. The software usually presents a screen image of a worksheet with columns and rows. The auditor can enter the same three basic types of data in the electronic worksheet, numbers, words, and formulas that the auditor could enter in a manual worksheet with a pencil. The major difference is that the electronic spreadsheet will store the formulas and immediately compute answers based on data stored elsewhere in the worksheet. These answers can immediately be changed if the auditor makes corrections or changes to the underlying data which the formula is using even though the data may be stored elsewhere in the worksheet.

Table 6.3, Basic Electronic Worksheet, illustrates how a simple income statement can be converted to a common-size income statement with the use of a single formula. As partially illustrated in Table 6.3, there are some other specific functions which electronic worksheet software can perform to greatly reduce the time it takes an auditor to perform a task. The handy function illustrated is the copying of data or formulas at very high speed.

TABLE 6.3. Basic Electronic Worksheet.

	1988	Formula	Common-Size Percentage
Revenues:			
Sales	$4,678,321	+E7/$E$10	0.93
Other Income	349,650	+E8/$E$10	0.07
	5,027,971	+E10/$E$10	1.00
Expenses:			
Cost of Goods Sold	2,675,865	+E12/$E$10	0.53
Marketing Expenses	675,433	+E13/$E$10	0.13
Administrative Expenses	890,768	+E14/$E$10	0.18
Interest Expense	432,333	+E15/$E$10	0.09
Other Expenses	165,456	+E16/$E$10	0.03
Income Tax Expense	289,755	+E17/$E$10	0.06
	4,242,066	+E19/$E$10	0.84
Net Income	$785,905	+E21/$E$10	0.16

(Note: The $ sign in the formula permanently fixes the denominator as location E10 [total revenues] in the worksheet.)

Thus, as in Table 6.3, an auditor can create a formula to compute common-size percentages and this formula can be copied for the entire income statement with only a few keystrokes. The computer software uses a concept called "relative address," meaning relative position in terms of column and row location of formula in worksheet, when copying a formula of the type illustrated. When the formula is copied to the worksheet location immediately below where the formula is originally created in the worksheet the software automatically adjusts the data locations specified in the original formula by one place. This means the formula that is created by copying, appropriately works on data located one place further down in the worksheet.

Another convenient function is that the software can store a series of keystrokes (commands) commonly called a "macro" and will perform them when the auditor pushes a single key. This can save a great deal of time for repetitive tasks. For example, the auditor can store all the keystrokes (commands) needed to print out a common-size statement. Then, when the auditor wants to print a copy of the common-size statement, pressing a single key produces a printout.

The ability to create custom menus to guide people using the electronic worksheet who are unfamiliar with the software is another handy feature. A custom menu is a listing of program choices that a program user can select. Since this menu simplifies the user options it will greatly increase productivity if electronic worksheet software is going to be accessed and used by a wide variety of individuals who are not familiar with all the program features.

Another advantage of electronic spreadsheet software is that a large number of interrelated documents can be stored in a single worksheet thus facilitating the sharing of data even though the documents may be treated as separate for printing and other purposes. For example, version 2.01 of Lotus 1-2-3™, one of the most popular software packages of this type, can hold 256 columns and 8192 rows of data in a single worksheet. This is roughly equivalent to 300 pages of 8.5 × 11 inch workpaper. Thus, an auditor could have, theoretically, 300 pages of related audit worksheets stored in a single template where all the numbers and formulas are interrelated. This means that an auditor could have a working trial balance with complete balance sheet and income statement data stored in one part of the electronic worksheet and enter the formulas necessary for different types of analytical auditing in a different part of the same worksheet.

This concept is illustrated in Figure 6.1, Different functional areas in an electronic worksheet. The row and column space occupied by the functional area may be determined by reading the column letters above the worksheet and the row numbers to the left side of the worksheet. It is assumed that each functional area occupies 8 columns and 45 lines of space. For example, the worksheet index occupies the space from A1 to H45. The balance sheet to the right of the worksheet index occupies the space from I1 to P45. The working trial balance which is below the worksheet index occupies the space from A46 to H90. The space depicted in Figure 6.1 is much smaller than the maximum space available in a typical electronic worksheet and only represents what would be six different manual worksheets stored in one electronic worksheet. If we attempt to visualize the broadest application of the concept of several different schedules or working papers sharing part of one large electronic worksheet, we arrive at the notion that all working papers potentially can be in an electronic worksheet and that manual working papers will be eliminated. This approach will undoubtedly be implemented by some auditing firms within the next decade.

When interrelated schedules are stored in the same electronic worksheet each schedule is updated when data in any other schedule is changed. This means that when an adjustment is posted to the adjusting entry schedule, the balances in all other schedules that contain those ac-

```
A B C D E F G H I J K L M N O P Q R S T U V W X
```

1		
2		
3 WORKSHEET	BALANCE	INCOME
. INDEX	SHEET	STATEMENT
.		
.		
.		
46		
47 WORKING	COMMON	COMMON
48		
. TRIAL	SIZE	SIZE
.		
. BALANCE	BALANCE SHEET	INCOME STATEMENT
91		
92		
93 ADJUSTING	FINANCIAL	STATEMENT OF
. JOURNAL	RATIO	CASH
. ENTRIES	ANALYSIS	FLOWS
.		
135		

Figure 6.1. Different functional areas in an electronic worksheet.

counts will be immediately changed. For example, suppose we entered in the adjusting entry schedule an adjusting entry debiting Uncollectible Accounts Expense for $10,000 and credit Accounts Receivable for $10,000. The balance sheet and income statement schedules would both be immediately updated for the changed balances. Additionally, any ratios in the financial ratio schedule, such as the current ratio, that utilized data from either of the two accounts adjusted would be immediately updated. Also, the percentage for accounts receivable in the common-size balance sheet schedule and the percentage for uncollectible accounts expense in the common-size income statement schedule would be immediately changed to reflect the adjusting entry.

Many electronic worksheet software packages permit the auditor to create a "window" to view different parts of the worksheet simultaneously. This simply means that the auditor can divide the computer's viewing screen into different sections called "windows" and look at a different part of the worksheet in each "window." This is extremely helpful since, as noted previously, an electronic worksheet could be as big as 300 8.5 × 11 inch pages which is much too much to view on a single computer screen. "Windows" can also facilitate data analysis. For example, an auditor could have data listed on one part of the computer display and be examining a graph of that data on another part of the display screen. This type of application takes advantage of another feature of microcomputers and electronic worksheet packages, the ability of the software to draw graphs and fit lines to the data in the graphs. In fact, this is only one of many data manipulation capabilities that such software has. All five of the techniques discussed in Chapter 4 can be automated by electronic worksheet software. Table 6.4, Two Simple Trend Analysis Approaches, illustrates two of these techniques as applied to a five-year set of time-series data in an electronic worksheet format.

TABLE 6.4. Two Simple Trend Analysis Approaches.

TIME SERIES DATA

Year	1984	1985	1986	1987	1988	1989 Projected	1989 Actual	$ Diff From Projected	% Diff From Projected
Sales	135000	154000	191000	234000	276000	?	326000	?	?

WEIGHTED AVERAGE CHANGE METHOD

Year	Sales	Change	Weight	Chg * Wgt
1984	135000			
1985	154000	19000	1 / 10	1900
1986	191000	37000	2 / 10	7400
1987	234000	43000	3 / 10	12900
1988	276000	42000	4 / 10	16800
			Sum	39000
			1988 Sales	276000
			Projected	315000

						315000	326000	11000	3.49

WEIGHTED MOVING AVERAGE

		A	B	C	B + C				
Year	Sales	.7 Times Sales	.3 Times Prior Forecast	Forecast For Next Year					
1984	135000	94500	40500	135000					
1985	154000	107800	40500	148300					
1986	191000	133700	44490	178190					
1987	234000	163800	53457	217257					
1988	276000	193200	65177	258377	258377	326000	-67623	-26.17	
1989	326000								

REFERENCES

Ewing, D. P. *1.2.3. Macro Library.* Indianapolis, Indiana: Que Corporation, 1985.

Kunitake, W. K., A. D. Luzi, and G. W. Glezen. "Analytical Review for Audit and Review Engagements," *The CPA Journal* (April 1985): 18-26.

Lotus Development Corporation. *1-2-3 Reference Manual*—Release 2. Cambridge, Massachusetts: Lotus Development Corporation, 1985.

McKee, T. E. *Analytical Techniques for Audit or Review Purposes* (CPE coursebook). New York: AICPA, 1987.

Zimmerman, S. M., and L. M. Conrad. *Understanding and Using Microcomputers.* St. Paul, Minnesota: West Publishing Company, 1986.

7
Using Industry Data to Extend Basic Analyses

The problem of establishing an appropriate norm against which to compare the results of analytical auditing procedures may be approached in yet another fashion, use of industry data. Industry data provides a benchmark against which the results of many types of analysis may be compared. This chapter discusses industry data advantages, uses or types of analyses, sources, and disadvantages in analytical auditing.

ADVANTAGES OF USING INDUSTRY DATA

Industry data offers the opportunity to enhance many analytical auditing techniques. Use of external comparative industry data can have the advantages of normative or theoretical value, independence, and advance warning. We will briefly discuss each of these potential advantages.

We previously mentioned that financial theory is not sufficiently developed to provide norms or standards for most financial relationships. In the absence of theoretical norms, the primary value of industry data is that it can provide norms of another type. In fact, industry statistics are sometimes presumed to be the "ideal" benchmark or standard toward which companies should strive. This presumption is created because of the definition of what constitutes an industry. An industry may be defined as being a group of companies supplying a similar set of products in the same market. We would expect that companies in an individual industry would be more similar in more respects (e.g., similar product inputs, distribution methods, or production methods) than companies in a different industry. Thus companies in the same industry should be more directly comparable than companies generally. This corresponds somewhat to a theoretical model that posits that only economy-wide factors, industry-wide factors, and firm-specific factors cause differences in individual ratios or financial relationships. Industry ratios presumably would reflect both the economy- and industry-wide factors thus isolating through a comparative analysis any firm-specific factors that might exist. Auditors would, of course, want to identify any firm-specific factors. If there are no firm-specific factors, then an individual company and industry ratio should closely correspond in the absence of any errors or irregularities in the firm's financial data.

Another advantage of industry data is that it is derived from an independent source. Data developed independently of the firm being audited potentially provides stronger audit evidence than analyses made solely with an individual firm's data which could be deliberately biased. This is consistent with a basic auditing theory evidential concept which holds that evidence from sources external to the auditee is generally stronger than internal evidence.

Industry data also offers the advantage of advance warning. Some firms consistently lag industry activities. If an auditor establishes that such a relationship exists then knowledge of current industry events can provide the auditor with advance information about what may happen to the firm.

TYPES OF INDUSTRY DATA ANALYSES

Industry data may be used in all types of analytical auditing previously discussed in this book. The effectiveness in using industry data, however, tends to vary with both the technique employed and the quality of industry data used. Some techniques are better suited for the use of industry data than are other techniques. Industry data can vary greatly in terms of quality and significance, both of which will be discussed in more detail later in this chapter.

One use of industry data is with the Current Period to Prior Period Change Method of simple trend analysis. In performing this type of analysis an auditor must, at a minimum, know the direction of the industry data in order to evaluate the reasonableness of the change in the company being audited. Preferably the auditor would know both the direction and amount of industry change for each account being evaluated by this method. The direction and change information is usually expressed in common-size percentages. The auditor's analysis for an individual account, for example sales, might be as follows:

	Prior Year	Current Year	Change	Difference
Company Sales	1.41	1.55	.14 ⎫	.10
Industry Sales	1.55	1.59	.04 ⎭	

The auditor would then have to evaluate whether a 10% difference was reasonable based on the company's normal relationship to the industry percentages. A difference of that magnitude might not be reasonable, in which case, the auditor would have to investigate the sales account appropriately. On the other hand, it might be normal for the company to lag industry sales which may have increased in the prior period. In the latter case, the 10% difference could be reasonable if the company experienced a sales increase in the current period that the majority of the industry experienced in the previous period. The auditor would have to determine what the company's relationship to industry changes would normally be.

Figure 7.1, Graphical analysis—with industry data, illustrates how the graphical method of simple trend analysis can provide an excellent background method for providing the auditor with information about a company's relation to the industry. As evident in Figure 7.1, the company lags the industry by four to five quarters as both go through what appears to be a cycle occurring every twelve quarters. The graphical method is frequently employed with industry data in a carry-forward schedule similar to Figure 7.1. This type of schedule is useful for audit planning purposes. It can provide an auditor with general information about the company that the auditor may need to properly perform or evaluate other audit procedures.

The Average Change Method, Weighted Average Method, and Weighted Moving Average Methods of simple trend analysis also can be used with industry data. These techniques can solve a common problem that auditors frequently encounter in using industry data—the lack of industry data for the most recent period. Industry data for the most recent fiscal period is frequently not published close enough to the end of the fiscal period so that it can be used by an auditor auditing a company for the same fiscal period. There is invariably a time delay between collecting and publishing such data. The three simple trend projection techniques can be used to project industry data for the current fiscal period to establish a norm against which to compare the company being audited. Since industry data is an average of many different data sets it is usually somewhat easier to project than single company data since much of the variability inherent in such individual data is smoothed out in the industry average.

Another highly popular application of industry data is in performing ratio analysis. The industry data provides a useful comparison base or

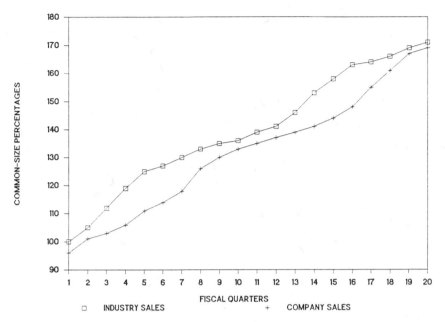

Figure 7.1. Graphical analysis—with industry data.

norm for most ratios. If industry data is obtained and used only for the current year under audit then this type of analysis is cross-sectional analysis where the industry data for the year becomes the norm. This type of application is illustrated here for the inventory turnover ratio:

Ratio	Company Ratio	Industry Ratio	Difference
Inventory Turnover	5.6	6.5	−.9 or −14%

If the industry ratio were regarded as an appropriate norm for comparison then the difference could indicate a problem in the inventory area, such as excess inventory. Many companies, however, may move in the same direction as their industry changes but may exhibit continuing patterns of difference with respect to the industry ratios. If this were true in the previous example then the auditor might not be able to directly use the industry ratio as an appropriate norm.

An analytical auditing procedure that helps with the problem discussed in the preceding paragraph is a time-series analysis of both the company and industry ratio. This type of analysis can alert the auditor to continuing differences that the company may exhibit with respect to industry ratios.

Figure 7.2, Graphical analysis—industry and company turnover ratios, illustrates such an analysis as applied to inventory turnover. It is obvious from the graph that the company has historically exhibited an inventory turnover ratio which has averaged approximately one turn less than the industry average. This analysis would indicate to the auditor analyzing the inventory turnover difference of −.9 in the preceding paragraph that the difference was reasonable based on the time-series analysis. This would mean that no special questions about the inventory account were raised by the analytical auditing procedure.

Industry data may also be used to analyze common-size financial statements. In fact, as noted previously, one common format for industry data is in a common-size format. Table 7.1, Industry Financial Ratios, illustrates the type of common-size industry data that is frequently available. In Table 7.1, the five columns on the right provide common-size industry data for the preceding five years. The five columns on the left in Table 7.1 provide current year common-size industry data for four different company sizes and for the industry overall.

Industry data is frequently coded by standard industry classification (SIC) number. This is a four digit code described in the *Standard Industrial Classification Manual* (Office of Management and Budget) that is used to classify all companies by the type of industry or activity they engage in.

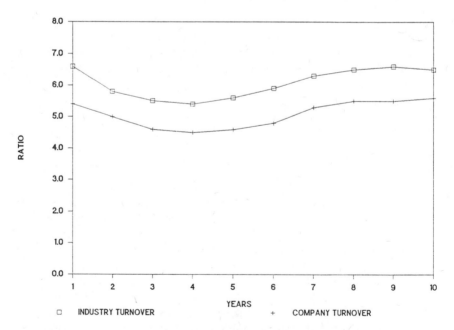

Figure 7.2. Graphical analysis—industry and company turnover ratios.

TABLE 7.1. Industry Financial Ratios.

MANUFACTURERS - ELECTRONIC COMPONENTS & ACCESSORIES SIC# 3671 (72-79)

Current Data					Type of Statement	Comparative Historical Data				
10	107	71	17	205	Unqualified			253	229	205
8	6	1	1	15	Qualified			15	19	15
47	49	3	1	100	Reviewed	DATA NOT AVAILABLE		109	79	100
32	33	3		68	Compiled			71	57	68
22	31	11	3	67	Other			71	74	67
214(6/30-9/30/86)		241(10/1/86-3/31/87)				6/30/82-3/31/83	6/30/83-3/31/84	6/30/84-3/31/85	6/30/85-3/31/86	6/30/86-3/31/87
0-1MM	1-10MM	10-50MM	50-100MM	ALL	**ASSET SIZE**	ALL	ALL	ALL	ALL	ALL
111	228	94	22	455	**NUMBER OF STATEMENTS**	413	460	519	458	455
%	%	%	%	%	**ASSETS**	%	%	%	%	%
7.9	8.9	11.4	10.8	9.2	Cash & Equivalents	8.9	9.4	8.1	8.7	9.2
35.0	27.7	20.6	17.6	27.6	Trade Receivables - (net)	27.4	28.7	29.0	26.3	27.6
24.9	27.2	22.6	19.3	25.3	Inventory	26.5	26.7	28.1	27.8	25.3
2.2	2.1	2.6	3.6	2.3	All Other Current	2.2	2.6	2.3	2.7	2.3
70.0	65.8	57.4	51.2	64.4	Total Current	64.9	67.4	67.5	65.5	64.4
22.9	27.7	33.9	34.1	28.1	Fixed Assets (net)	27.9	26.2	26.0	27.5	28.1
1.1	1.4	1.4	3.7	1.4	Intangibles (net)	.9	.6	1.0	1.3	1.4
6.1	5.1	7.3	11.1	6.1	All Other Non-Current	6.3	5.8	5.5	5.7	6.1
100.0	100.0	100.0	100.0	100.0	Total	100.0	100.0	100.0	100.0	100.0
					LIABILITIES					
11.5	10.2	7.6	7.4	9.8	Notes Payable-Short Term	9.0	10.0	9.0	10.0	9.8
6.0	4.9	3.0	1.9	4.6	Cur. Mat-L/T/D	3.3	3.4	3.4	3.5	4.6
15.5	13.4	8.7	7.3	12.7	Trade Payables	13.6	14.7	14.3	12.6	12.7
1.2	1.4	1.3	.4	1.3	Income Taxes Payable	–	–	2.0	1.3	1.3
9.5	8.4	7.8	8.2	8.5	All Other Current	11.9	12.2	10.4	9.1	8.5
43.7	38.2	28.3	25.3	36.9	Total Current	37.9	40.3	39.1	36.4	36.9
15.3	15.1	19.1	20.9	16.3	Long Term Debt	14.7	13.4	14.4	15.5	16.3
.1	.6	1.7	2.0	.8	Deferred Taxes	–	–	.9	1.0	.8
2.8	2.9	2.9	7.2	3.1	All Other Non-Current	3.3	2.7	2.7	2.4	3.1
38.1	43.2	47.9	44.6	43.0	Net Worth	44.1	43.5	42.9	44.7	43.0
100.0	100.0	100.0	100.0	100.0	Total Liabilities & Net Worth	100.0	100.0	100.0	100.0	100.0
					INCOME DATA					
100.0	100.0	100.0	100.0	100.0	Net Sales	100.0	100.0	100.0	100.0	100.0
37.9	33.3	29.7	32.4	33.6	Gross Profit	33.4	35.0	34.4	34.2	33.6
34.4	29.3	27.5	27.3	30.0	Operating Expenses	27.4	27.8	26.6	28.9	30.0
3.5	4.1	2.2	5.1	3.6	Operating Profit	6.0	7.1	7.8	5.3	3.6
.9	1.4	1.4	1.5	1.3	All Other Expenses (net)	1.7	1.0	1.1	1.3	1.3
2.6	2.6	.8	3.6	2.3	Profit Before Taxes	4.3	6.1	6.6	4.0	2.3
					RATIOS					
2.4	2.7	3.5	3.8	2.9	Current	2.8	2.7	2.7	3.1	2.9
1.6	1.7	2.3	2.1	1.8		1.8	1.7	1.8	1.9	1.8
1.2	1.3	1.6	1.5	1.3		1.3	1.2	1.3	1.3	1.3
1.7	1.4	2.0	2.2	1.6	Quick	1.5	1.5	1.5	1.6	1.6
1.0	1.0 (93)	1.3	1.0 (454)	1.0		1.0	1.0	1.0	1.0 (454)	1.0
.6	.7	.8	.7	.7		.6	.6	.7	.6	.7
38 9.7	44 8.3	49 7.4	49 7.5	43 8.5	Sales/Receivables	41 8.9	46 8.0	44 8.3	42 8.6	43 8.5
49 7.5	53 6.9	59 6.2	73 5.0	54 6.7		54 6.8	59 6.2	56 6.5	51 7.1	54 6.7
58 6.3	66 5.6	76 4.8	87 4.2	68 5.4		68 5.4	74 4.9	70 5.2	66 5.4	68 5.4
31 11.8	47 7.7	59 6.2	78 4.7	45 8.1	Cost of Sales/Inventory	44 8.3	50 7.3	47 7.7	47 7.7	45 8.1
56 6.5	76 4.8	99 3.7	126 2.9	76 4.8		79 4.6	83 4.4	86 4.3	85 4.3	76 4.8
104 3.5	126 2.9	152 2.4	192 1.9	130 2.8		130 2.8	135 2.7	130 2.8	140 2.6	130 2.8
16 22.3	20 18.0	23 16.1	24 15.2	20 18.2	Cost of Sales/Payables	22 16.7	24 15.5	23 15.9	21 17.3	20 18.2
35 10.4	35 10.4	33 11.0	38 9.6	35 10.4		33 10.9	39 9.3	38 9.7	34 10.8	35 10.4
53 6.9	56 6.5	52 7.0	60 6.1	55 6.6		55 6.6	61 6.0	56 6.5	50 7.3	55 6.6
6.0	3.8	2.3	2.1	3.6	Sales/Working Capital	3.8	3.6	3.9	3.4	3.6
10.1	7.1	4.4	3.4	6.8		7.2	6.9	7.0	5.9	6.8
27.3	16.5	8.6	7.8	16.3		18.7	18.8	14.8	14.7	16.3
(99) 7.4	(195) 7.5	(79) 6.1	(19) 6.3	(392) 7.1	EBIT/Interest	(349) 8.6	(398) 8.6	(447) 11.0	(409) 8.3	(392) 7.1
2.4	2.8	2.3	1.4	2.6		3.1	3.7	4.6	3.1	2.6
.5	1.2	-.8	-2.1	.6		1.0	1.6	2.0	.8	.6
(63) 4.9	(159) 6.5	(66) 10.5	(18) 20.5	(306) 7.1	Net Profit + Depr., Dep., Amort./Cur. Mat. L/T/D	(270) 8.7	(304) 9.5	(354) 9.0	(322) 8.8	(306) 7.1
1.4	2.5	2.6	3.5	2.2		3.3	3.2	4.0	2.8	2.2
.4	1.2	.9	-1.4	1.0		1.4	1.6	2.1	1.1	1.0
.2	.3	.4	.4	.3	Fixed/Worth	.3	.3	.3	.3	.3
.6	.6	.6	.9	.6		.6	.6	.6	.6	.6
1.7	1.2	1.3	1.5	1.3		1.1	1.1	1.1	1.1	1.3
.8	.7	.4	.7	.7	Debt/Worth	.6	.6	.7	.6	.7
1.7	1.4	1.1	1.2	1.4		1.3	1.4	1.4	1.3	1.4
4.2	2.7	2.2	2.5	2.8		2.5	2.7	2.7	2.4	2.8
(102) 40.8	(221) 32.4	(89) 23.9	(21) 30.6	(433) 33.0	% Profit Before Taxes/Tangible Net Worth	(401) 39.0	(452) 46.7	(507) 52.8	(438) 35.0	(433) 33.0
19.5	13.9	9.4	19.2	14.2		21.0	24.4	28.5	16.8	14.2
2.0	3.2	-11.9	-6.2	.5		2.5	6.2	10.0	.6	.5
17.5	12.7	12.8	12.3	13.7	% Profit Before Taxes/Total Assets	17.2	15.9	20.7	16.2	13.7
6.4	5.4	3.9	5.4	5.3		9.3	9.0	11.5	7.5	5.3
-.7	.7	-5.6	-3.4	-1.1		-.2	2.6	3.9	-.4	-1.1
28.7	14.5	5.9	5.0	14.5	Sales/Net Fixed Assets	13.4	14.1	14.4	13.4	14.5
13.4	7.6	3.7	3.1	6.8		7.0	7.0	7.6	7.3	6.8
6.3	4.3	2.4	2.0	3.5		4.0	3.9	4.4	4.2	3.5
3.1	2.4	1.4	1.3	2.4	Sales/Total Assets	2.3	2.3	2.4	2.3	2.4
2.4	1.8	1.1	.8	1.7		1.8	1.8	1.9	1.7	1.7
1.8	1.4	.9	.7	1.2		1.3	1.3	1.4	1.3	1.2
(101) 1.4	(202) 1.9	(81) 2.7	(18) 3.9	(402) 1.9	% Depr., Dep., Amort./Sales	(376) 1.6	(415) 1.6	(462) 1.7	(415) 1.8	(402) 1.9
2.4	3.1	4.3	4.6	3.4		2.7	2.7	2.8	3.0	3.4
4.1	5.2	7.5	6.7	5.4		4.5	4.2	3.9	4.9	5.4
(43) 3.7	(49) 2.9		(94) 3.4		% Officers' Comp/Sales	(112) 3.1	(116) 3.0	(138) 3.2	(110) 3.5	(94) 3.4
7.1	4.7		5.7			5.4	5.7	5.7	5.7	5.7
11.7	7.9		9.7			8.6	9.1	9.4	8.1	9.7
150921M	1373713M	2422912M	1565947M	5513493M	Net Sales ($)	5294729M	5685665M	8548212M	6608945M	5513493M
62920M	782399M	2135791M	1828027M	4609137M	Total Assets ($)	3994201M	4281380M	5885645M	5034487M	4609137M

©Robert Morris Associates 1987   M = $thousand   MM = $million

Source: Robert Morris Associates. Annual Statement Studies (Philadelphia, Pennsylvania: 1987) Page 102, © 1987 by Robert Morris Associates. Reprinted by permission.

The codes encompass all types of economic activity. They are intended to facilitate the collection and dissemination of statistical data. It is possible to use only the first two or three digits of the four digit numbers if less specialized industry information is desired. A two-digit number is the broadest classification of an industry while a four-digit number is the narrowest. A two digit number, for example, would describe a general industry classification, such as food products, while a four digit number with the same first two digits would describe a specialized portion of the same general industry classification, such as malt beverages. If a company's product line encompasses two or more different industries then use of a single SIC number to classify the overall company based on its dominant business activity could be misleading since several different SIC numbers could be used to classify portions of the company.

Table 7.1 also contains some industry financial ratios in addition to the common-size financial statement percentages. The sixteen ratios listed there may not include all the ratios for which an auditor would like industry ratios. It is possible for an auditor to use the industry asset and sales totals contained on the last line in Table 7.1 along with the common-size statement percentages to construct some additional ratios. For example, suppose the auditor wanted to compute the industry Net Worth To Sales ratio (owners' equity/sales). The auditor could take the industry sales and asset totals and divide them by the number of companies in the industry to get average sales and assets for the industry. The common-size percentage for owners' equity could then be applied to the average industry assets to compute the average industry owner's equity. The ratio could then be directly computed as in the following illustration:

	Assets	Sales
A. Industry totals	$5,034,487,000	$6,508,945,000
B. Number of Companies in Industry	458	458
C. Industry averages (A/B)	$10,992,330	$14,211,015
D. Owners' equity common-size percentages	44.7%	

Industry owner's equity to sales $(.447 \times 10{,}992{,}330)/14{,}211{,}015 = .35$

This illustrates that an auditor may have to make some computations with industry data in order to extract the desired information since industry data may not always be provided in a format most useful to an auditor.

SOURCES OF INDUSTRY DATA

There are quite a variety of possible sources for obtaining industry data. Some data is better suited for the auditors' use than others. An auditor must be familiar with the type of industry data, the method for obtaining it, and subsequent processing in order to evaluate how much reliance to place on the data. For example, an auditor would normally place less reliance on industry data that was compiled from unaudited (as compared to audited) financial statement data. One of the best sources for industry data is from industry trade associations. They frequently collect, compile, and disseminate industry data as a service to their members. This data is published in the industry trade journal on a regular basis. If an auditor is not familiar with the trade associations and related journals in a particular industry, client personnel can usually advise. In order to encourage the sharing of individual company data with other members of the industry, the industry trade associations sometimes restrict access to the data they have collected to those members who have provided data for the study. Industry trade data of this type is usually quite good and may provide more specific detailed information than that available from other sources. Some examples of industry trade associations that publish industry data include:

- National Farm and Power Equipment Dealers' Association
- National Electrical Contractors' Association
- National Office Products Association
- National Association of Textile and Apparel Wholesalers
- National Restaurant Association
- National Electric Manufacturers
- American Trucking Association, Inc.
- National Retail Merchants' Association
- American Retail Hardware Association
- National Wholesaler Druggist Association
- American Meat Institute
- American Paper Institute

Another source of industry data is "pseudo-industry statistics" constructed by the auditor. In this approach the auditor selects some competitors of the client being audited and computes a norm from their financial information. This approach was illustrated in Table 6.2 in the previous chapter. Although this method can be time consuming if it is difficult to identify competitors or obtain their statements, it offers a significant advantage. Since the auditor is making the selection, the companies selected can be closely matched with the auditee thus perhaps achieving greater similarity than would be obtained from normal industry statistics. The auditor can also assign different weights to the various competitors to obtain an even better match. Identification of actual or potential competitors can sometimes be accomplished through the use of product directories. These directories typically publish information by company name, service, product name, and trade name. Two examples of product directories are *The Thomas Register of American Manufacturers* and *MacRae's Bluebook.*

Although industry data is normally in a printed media it is becoming increasingly common to find it also available in a computer database. These databases are established and maintained either by the trade associations or by commercial vendors whose primary business is the selling of database services. To obtain this data an auditor needs a microcomputer with a modem and authorized access to the database. The auditor simply dials the database over regular telephone lines and downloads (copies into the auditor's computer's memory) the data. One advantage of this method is that the industry data may be more current than the published data. Also, this method is very fast and if the auditor is using a significant amount of industry data there can be significant time savings. The cost is usually quite reasonable if the auditor uses the database regularly.

Other sources of industry data are:

* Dun and Bradstreet, Inc., Business Economics Division. *Key Business Ratios and Cost of Doing Business Series.*
* Robert Morris Associates. *Annual Statement Studies.*
* Moody's Investor Service. *Moody's Industrial Manual.*
* *The Bank of New York Comparative Ratio Study.*
* *Almanac of Business and Industrial Financial Ratios* by Leo Troy, Prentice-Hall, Inc.
* *Financial Studies of Small Business.* Financial Research Associates.
* Standard and Poor' Corporation. *Standard and Poor's Industry Surveys.*
* U.S. Internal Revenue Service. *Statistics of Income.*
* Federal Deposit Insurance Corporation. *Bank Operating Statistics.*
* Harris, Kerr, Foster & Company. *Trends in the Hotel–Motel Business.*
* Laventhol, Krekstein, Horwath & Horwath. *Restaurants, Country Clubs, City Clubs: Report on Operations.*
* Printing Industries of America. *Ratios for Use of Printing Management.*
* Federal Trade Commission. *Manufacturing, Mining, and Trade Corporations Financial Data and Ratios.*
* U. S. Department of Commerce. Wide range of financial and operating statistics.
* Institute of Real Estate Management, Experience Exchange Committee. *A Statistical Compilation and Analysis of Actual Income and Expenses Experienced In Apartments, Condominiums and Cooperative Building Operation.*

Much of the printed industry data previously noted, plus numerous other statistical sources and government statistics not mentioned, are available, for example, in university libraries. Two excellent references which assist in accessing these statistics are *Statistical Sources* and *Statistical Services of the United States Government.*

LIMITATIONS OF INDUSTRY DATA

There are a number of potential problems associated with using industry data to perform analytical auditing procedures. An auditor must be aware of these potential problems in order to reasonably evaluate and deal with them.

One significant problem can be classifying a company into an appropriate industry. This is not usually a problem for a small single product or service company. However, a larger multi-product or multi-service company may not "fit" very well in a single industry classification. For example, a company that derives 53% of its revenues from the sale of computer parts and 47% of its revenues from the sale of financial services may be classified by SIC number as primarily a retailer of computer parts. Its financial data will not compare very well with other retailers of computer parts whose business is 100% computer parts sales. One solution to this problem is to analyze the data at the product line level rather than the overall company level. This approach can usually be easily implemented when the overall company is simply a consolidation of individual operating companies. It may not work as well for entities which do not employ separate operating companies for the various product lines. In this latter case, income statement data may be available by product line but balance sheet data may not be. A second possible solution to the problem of appropriately classifying a company is the previously discussed approach of the auditor constructing some "pseudo" industry statistics from competitors who would have the same industry mix within their companies.

Another problem with using industry data is that, even within fairly narrow industry categories, the companies that comprise the industry may be very dissimilar in many respects. For example, they may use different accounting principles that make their results less comparable. They may be in different geographical regions which could change their cost structure due to freight or operating cost differences. Also, they may have a different financial structure which could change their results significantly. The subsidiary of a large conglomerate may maintain a different level of current assets or buy materials from the conglomerate at a different price than an independently owned and run company. These differences within an industry can reduce the effectiveness of the industry data as an audit tool. There is some empirical research indicating certain industry ratios may not differ that much across different industries because of the variability of data within individual industries due to some of the factors previously discussed. If the industry ratios do not differ that much across different industries then that means they may be of limited value as a comparison base in analytical auditing. Industry data with a high degree of variability can usually be identified if the auditor obtains industry statistics which indicate the variability within the industry. Variability can be indicated by data giving the range over which an individual ratio varies. The Robert Morris Associates Data in Table 7.1 includes the upper and lower quartiles for the individual ratios listed there. The lower quartile is the point where the ratios of the firms classified at the 25 percentile would fall (only 25% of the firms would have a ratio lower than this). The upper quartile is the point where the ratios of the firms classified at the 75 percentile would fall (only 25% of the firms would have a ratio higher than this). Suppose we found the two different industries with the following debt to equity ratios:

	Industry A	Industry B
Upper Quartile	1.1	.1
Median	1.3	1.3
Lower Quartile	1.5	2.9

The quartile variability from the median in Industry A is only 15%—$(1.3 - 1.1)/1.3$. The quartile variability from the median in Industry B is 92%—$(1.3 - .1)/1.3$. The Industry A ratio would appear to have a low enough variability to have significant predictive power while that does not appear to be the case in Industry B. An auditor confronted with Industry B might be better off constructing "pseudo" industry statistics from similar companies rather than using the published industry statistics.

Another potential problem with some industry statistics is the statistical unreliability of the sample from which the industry data is obtained. The sample may not be large enough or randomly selected. Auditors using industry data should evaluate the data selection method and determine that enough companies are reported to be appropriately representative of the industry.

REFERENCES

Blocher, E., and J. J. Willingham. *Analytical Review—A Guide to Evaluating Financial Statements.* New York: McGraw Hill Book Company, 1985.

Dedyo, H. P. *MacRae's Blue Book.* Hinsdale, Illinois: MacRae's Blue Book Service, 1987.

Foster, G. *Financial Statement Analysis.* New Jersey: Prentice-Hall, Inc., 1978.

Gupta, M. C., and R. J. Huefner. "A Cluster Analysis of Financial Ratios and Industry Characteristics," *Journal of Accounting Research* (Spring 1972): 77-95.

Kunitake, W. K., A. D. Luzi, and G. W. Glezen. "Analytical Review for Audit and Review Engagements," *The CPA Journal* (April 1985): 18-26.

McKee, T. E. *Analytical Techniques for Audit or Review Purposes* (CPE coursebook). New York: AICPA, 1987.

Neumann, F. E., "The Auditor's Analytical Review—Some Sources of Information," *The Journal of Accountancy* (October 1974): 88-92.

O'Brien, J. W. and S. R. Wasserman (Editors). *Statistical Sources* (Eleventh edition). Detroit: Gale Research Company, 1988.

Sanzo, R. *Ratio Analysis for Small Business,* 3rd ed. U. S. Small Business Administration, 1970.

Executive Office of the President—Office of Management and Budget. *Standard Industrial Classification Manual.* Washington, D.C.: Office of Management and Budget, 1987.

Thomas Publishing Company. *The Thomas Register of American Manufacturers.* 461 Eighth Avenue, New York, N.Y. 10001.

Trapnell, J. E. "An Empirical Study of the Descriptive Nature of Financial Ratios Relative to Industry Operating Characteristics," unpublished Ph.D. thesis, University of Georgia, Athens, 1977.

U.S. Office of Management and Budget—Statistical Policy Division. *Statistical Services of the United States Government* (Rev. Ed.). Washington, D.C.: U.S. Government Printing Office, 1975.

8
Simple Reasonableness Tests

The term "simple reasonableness test" is somewhat inappropriate in describing the type of analytical procedures discussed in this chapter. A more descriptive term might be a "nonstatistical structural model" which would permit us to distinguish from the "statistical structural models" discussed in the last chapter in this book. The problem with the term "simple reasonableness test" is that all analytical auditing procedures are reasonableness tests and many of them could be deemed "simple" if that term is deemed to mean any nonadvanced mathematical approach. For example, the Current Period To Prior Period simple trend analysis model could be called a "simple reasonableness test." We will, however, use the term "simple reasonableness test" since most auditors are more familiar and comfortable with that term.

A simple reasonableness test is defined in this book to mean a nonadvanced mathematical approach to constructing a structural model of a financial relationship. A structural model is one which attempts to predict an account balance using factors that are related to or cause changes in the account balance. These factors may be financial and/or operating data. This definition excludes any type of time-series trend models. An example of a simple reasonableness test would be the computation of the expected amount of interest expense using factors such as average amount of notes payable outstanding, average interest rate, and average time period that notes payable were outstanding.

Performance of a simple reasonableness test requires completion of three basic steps. First, identify variables that are related to the account to be tested. Second, determine the appropriate relationship (model) between the variables and the account. Finally, combine the variables to produce an estimate of the account.

ADVANTAGES

The interest expense test in the previous example employed a model which simplified certain aspects of the real computation process since averages were used as opposed to exact amounts, rates, or periods. If the exact amount of notes payable outstanding, the exact interest rate, and the exact time period were used then this would not be an analytical auditing procedure involving a model but rather a reperformance auditing test. A reperformance test is an auditing procedure where an auditor reperforms or repeats the original accounting process in order to verify that the account balance is the result of the correct application of that process.

A reperformance procedure changes to a modeling procedure when an auditor starts making simplifying assumptions, such as an average interest rate, or alteration of the original accounting process. Simplifying assumptions are usually made in order to save time on the test. The simplifying assumption of an average interest rate would allow the auditor to eliminate many separate computations that may have been made in the original accounting process in the previous example. Alterations to the original accounting process may be made to save time but they are also made for effectiveness reasons if the auditor believes that the original accounting process could produce an error or is biased. For example, an original computation process used by the client for bad debts expense might have used actual bad debts in relation to total sales for the prior five years to compute the bad debt rate for the current year. The auditor may know that the mix of cash sales and credit sales has changed over the prior five years and may alter the client's computation process by computing a bad debt expense rate using only credit sales not total sales. The auditor would then be simultaneously testing the original client process and performing sensitivity analysis to see if a change in one of the parameters would produce a significant difference. Thus, one of the advantages of simple reasonableness tests is that they may be either more efficient or more effective than reperformance tests.

In order to appropriately perform a simple reasonableness test the auditor must carefully consider all financial and nonfinancial factors which might be relevant to modeling the financial relationship. This means that the auditor should acquire greater knowledge of the account or area than if some alternative type of test were to be performed. This greater knowledge may enable the auditor to be more effective in auditing the account than the auditor would be in performing an alternative type of test which did not require this higher level of knowledge.

For example, suppose an auditor were going to audit the fleet fuel expense account for a company and could use either a simple trend analysis technique or a simple reasonableness test to project the account. If an auditor used a simple trend analysis technique to project the account and noted a 6% increase in a year when sales were up 5% and inflation was up 3% the auditor might accept the 6% increase as reasonable. On the other hand, if the auditor used a simple reasonableness test to try to compute fleet fuel expense the auditor might consider factors such as number of vehicles, vehicle mileage, gas mileage per vehicle, and cost of fuel. An investigation of these factors could reveal that as a result of a cost reduction drive the company reduced, by 25%, the number of vehicles in its fleet at the beginning of the third quarter. This data might make the 6% increase in fleet fuel expense appear to be unreasonable. One could argue that this information should have been also known for the simple trend test. However, different types of tests will sometimes aid in uncovering information that might otherwise be missed or aid the auditor in appropriately associating information with an individual account other than the original account. It is not uncommon, due to the vast quantities of data involved with an audit, for information to come to light at some point in the audit which may not be appropriately associated with a particular account. For example, suppose the 25% fleet reduction were discovered during the audit procedures for the plant and equipment account. An auditor could overlook appropriately associating this information with the fleet expense account at the time a simple trend analysis was performed. Thus, one of the benefits of simple reasonableness tests is the greater knowledge acquired of the account.

AUDIT APPROACH

As stated earlier, a simple reasonableness test basically involves constructing an appropriate model for the account being audited. The detailed steps in this process would normally include:

- Identify factors which may cause or influence changes in the account.
- Identify appropriate assumptions related to the account.
- Evaluate assumptions for reasonableness and consistency.
- Identify changes in the business or environment it operates which may warrant changing the assumptions or introducing additional factors in the model.
- Formulate the appropriate model.
- Make a projection with the model for the current period.
- Compare the projected result with the actual result and evaluate the difference as previously discussed.

COMMON REASONABLENESS TESTS FOR THE INCOME STATEMENT

The most common type of reasonableness test uses a simple relationship between accounts and operating data to predict an account balance. Since income statement accounts are more directly related to operating data than balance sheet accounts this type of test is more applicable to revenue and expense accounts.

Table 8.1, Simple Reasonableness Test for Payroll Expense, provides an illustration of a simple reasonableness test. In it the average number of employees is extended by average payroll cost per employee to get estimated payroll cost by payroll category. The estimates for each category are then added to obtain the total estimated payroll for the year. The estimate is compared to the actual payroll expense and the auditor makes an assessment about the difference. Table 8.1 illustrates several elements of good working paper preparation which were discussed in Chapter 3.

A cost-effective audit strategy is to alternate simple reasonableness tests with detailed tests on a yearly or other regular basis. The detailed tests can provide the auditor with data which can be easily projected into the following year thus frequently eliminating the need for a detailed test in that subsequent period. The data in Table 8.1 indicates that this type of audit strategy was pursued. Apparently the auditor made a detailed test of the payroll account during the prior year and used the salary rates established then, adjusted for salary increases, to make the current year projection.

Although data may be unavailable or unreliable in some audit situations, in most audits the auditor can make a simple reasonableness projection of many revenue and expense accounts. Table 8.2, Revenue Account Relationships for Simple Reasonableness Tests, lists revenue accounts and some related factors which an auditor might want to consider.

A few examples of some common expense account relationships which may be sometimes used to perform simple reasonableness tests are:

Expense Account	Related Factors
Interest	Principal amount
	Time period
	Interest rate
	Payment penalties
Repairs and maintenance	Machine hours
	Age of machines
Fuel	Fuel consumption rate
	Activity (miles, hours, etc.)
Travel	Number of days
	Daily per diem rate

TABLE 8.1. Simple Reasonableness Test for Payroll Expense.

XYZ Company
Analytical Test of Payroll Expense
12/31/88

Reference ___PL41___
Prepared By ___TEM___
Reviewed By ___RWR___

	Number of Employees at 1/1/88	Number of Employees 12/31/88	Average Number of Employees For Year	Average Payroll Cost Per Employee	Estimated Payroll Cost For Category
SALARIES					
ADMINISTATIVE SALARIES	21 #	24 <	22.5	$34,232.11 -	$ 770,222.48
PRODUCTION SALARIES	46 #	54 <	50	$26,967.45 &	1,348,372.50
HOURLY PAYROLL					
PLANT A	223 #	211 <	217	$16,453.12 @	3,570,327.00
PLANT B	344 #	367 <	355.5	$16,453.12 @	5,849,084.20
DISTRIBUTION CENTER	23 #	25 <	24	$16,453.12 @	394,874.88

Total Estimated Payroll   11,932,881.26

1988 Payroll Expense Debits in General Ledger Prior To Allocations   12,187,112.30

Difference $ 254,231.04

Difference As A Percentage Of Estimated Payroll   2.13%

CONCLUSION:

Difference indicated by this test is not deemed to be significant due to the averages employed in this test. This test indicates that the amount of payroll expense recorded and allocated was reasonable. No additional work deemed necessary beyond that called for in initial audit plan.

TICKMARK LEGEND:

\#   Obtained from working paper PL32 in 12/31/87 audit file. This working paper had FICA Expense reconciled to W-2's mailed to employees.

<   Obtained from working paper PL35, FICA Expense comparison to W-2s, in 12/31/88 audit file.

@   Computed by multiplying 52 weeks by 40 hours per week by $7.9102. The hourly rate of $7.9102 was computed by averaging the hourly wage rates per current union contract at PF342 under assumption that there are approximately the same number of employees in each of the fourteen wage rate classification specified in the union contract. This assumption appears reasonable based on the distribution of employees in these classifications in the 12/31/87 payroll register. Per conversation with Fred W. Smith, payroll supervisor, no overtime was authorized during 1988 with the exception of a few hundred hours for some maintenance personnel.

-   Obtained by multiplying 1987 average salary rate of $30,839.73 for this category, as indicated detailed payroll test on PL43 in 1987 audit file, by 1.11. PF77 indicates board of directors authorized an 11% average salary increase during 1988 for this category, to be distributed as deemed appropriate by top management.

&   Obtained by multiplying 1987 average salary rate of $24,295.00 for this category, as indicated in detailed payroll test on PL43 in 1987 audit file, by 1.11. PF77 indicates board of directors authorized an 11% average salary increase during 1988 for this category, to be distributed as deemed appropriate by top management.

118

TABLE 8.2. Revenue Account Relationships for Simple Reasonableness Tests.

Industry	Item Being Tested	Overall Verification Procedure
Hotel	Room revenue	Occupancy statistics multiplied by average room rates should approximate room revenue.
Leasing	Lease revenue	Number of units multiplied by average rental should approximate lease revenue.
Professional service	Fees billed	Number of employees multiplied by utilisation percentage and charge rates should approximate fees billed.
Transport	Revenue	Fuel used can be used to derive mileage travelled, which can be related to average revenue per mile to assess reasonableness of recorded revenue.
Municipalities	Taxation revenue	Assessed values multiplied by mill rates should yield taxation revenue.
Laudromat	Working machine revenue	Water usage can be used to project revenues
Banking	Interest revenue	Average loans outstanding multiplied by the number of days outstanding x the average rate should approximate interest revenue.
Nonprofit associations of institutions	Revenue	Enrolment statistics times average tuition, membership fees times annual dues.
Baking	Sales	Ingredients usage can be used to project sales volumes.

Source: D.G. Smith. *Analytical Review*. (Toronto: Canadian Institute of Chartered Accountants) 1987: 65. Reprinted with Permission.

Expense Account	Related Factor
Sales salaries	Number of personnel
	Base salary
	Commission rate
	Sales
Wages	Time
	Overtime
	Idle time
	Number of employees
	Wage rates
Bad debts	Receivables age category
	Loss rate by age category
	Credit rating
Electricity	Square footage
	Degree days

Expense Account	Related Factor
Electricity (continued)	Historical rate per square foot Number of operating days Number of machines Machine hours Historical rate per machine hour
Cost of goods sold	Quantity sold Historical cost adjusted for inflation or price changes Production technology

SIMPLE REASONABLENESS TESTS FOR THE BALANCE SHEET

The balance sheet accounts reflect balances remaining after both income related transactions and management discretionary decisions as to the desired level of balances. They are, therefore, generally somewhat less predictable than the income statement accounts which reflect primarily operating activity. It is possible, however, to perform simple reasonableness tests for a number of them. The following list contains some examples.

Balance Sheet Account	Related Factors
Inventory	Prior year standard costs adjusted for inflation times quantity computed based on sales.
Accounts receivable	Varying percentages of several prior month's sales historical collection experience.
Accrued payroll	Days accrued times average daily payroll or subsequent period gross payroll.
Accounts payable	Multiple of inventory Varying percentage of cost of goods sold for previous months and future months based on historical payment experience.
Accrued warranty	Percentage of sales times historical cost of warranty claims adjusted for inflation.

ACCOUNT ROLL-FORWARDS

Another type of possible simple reasonableness test is an account roll-forward. This type of test is necessary when an account has been tested at an interim data and the auditor must have reasonable assurance that the year end balance is proper. For example, if an auditor makes a physical inventory observation and price test three months prior to fiscal year end the auditor will normally want some assurance that the year end balance is proper.

The normal structural format for an account roll-forward test is (1) interim balance that was tested, (2) plus monthly account increases, (3) less monthly account decreases, provides (4) new balance. The new balance computed may then be rolled forward to the second following month. This process may be repeated for as many months as necessary to arrive at the fiscal year-end balance.

The logic behind this type of test is that if the beginning balance was tested and the increases and decreases are tested then the new balance must be correct even though it is not directly tested. Although other audit procedures involving direct testing may be used to test the monthly increases and decreases, a common audit approach is to use either a trend analysis test or a simple reasonableness test to obtain assurance for these amounts.

A trend analysis approach involves making a projection of monthly increases or decreases to the account from the period that preceded the interim balance that was tested. These amounts will be either from the current year, and therefore unaudited, and/or be from the prior years, which would normally have been audited. If the physical inventory results in only small adjustments or none, the unaudited balances from the current year are normally assumed to be accurate enough for purposes of making a trend analysis projection based on the logic that they resulted in an accurate account balance. If there were very significant adjustments based on the interim physical inventory then the trend analysis projection should not be used since the previous assumption could not be made.

A simple reasonableness test approach involves using a simple reasonableness test to obtain assurance about the monthly account increases and decreases that have occurred since the interim date. Let us consider the inventory account for an example. The monthly increases in the inventory account for a merchandising business would normally result from the cost of goods sold. A simple reasonableness test might be to assume that these amounts would be equal unless inventory were normally increased or decreased in the particular month due to seasonal factors. A seasonal factor would be present if inventory normally increased 10% in October and 20% in November in anticipation of Christmas sales. Our simple reasonableness test for October inventory decreases, then, might be to compute the decrease as the appropriate cost of goods sold percentage of October sales. The simple reasonableness test for October inventory increases, then, might be to compute the increase as 110% of the appropriate cost of goods sold percentage of October sales. If purchase returns or sales returns and allowances were normally significant then these items could be adjusted in the computation as a percentage of cost of goods sold. The astute auditor will see that the simple reasonableness test just described is a variation on the gross margin method of inventory estimation in which the purchases are adjusted for seasonal patterns.

LIMITATIONS OF REASONABLENESS TESTS

One limitation of simple reasonableness tests is the difficulty sometimes encountered in trying to get reasonably reliable nonfinancial information to use for the tests. If an auditor has to spend a significant time constructing the data then it may be more cost-beneficial to perform some other type of test. Many organizations now have computerized data bases which contain many types of nonfinancial information which could be useful in performing this type of test. Controls over this data are sometimes not as good as controls over financial information. An auditor must be confident that such data is sufficiently reliable before using it in an audit test. If there are questions about data reliability then the auditor must test the data to establish its reliability.

Another problem with simple reasonableness tests is that it may be difficult for an auditor to appropriately identify the relationship (model) between an account and possible causal factors when there are two or more possible causal factors. For example, if electricity is used for heating, lighting, and powering production equipment it may be difficult to explicitly identify a relationship that will permit the auditor to calculate the estimated electricity expense. Relationships with two or more causal factors can sometimes be modeled with a statistical technique called regression analysis which is discussed in the next chapter.

REFERENCES

Blocher, E., and J. J. Willingham. *Analytical Review—A Guide to Evaluating Financial Statements.* New York: McGraw Hill Book Company, 1985.

Grobstein, M., S. E. Loeb, and R. D. Neary, *Auditing—A Risk Analysis Approach.* Homewood, Illinois: Richard D. Irwin, Inc., 1985.

Smith, D. G. *Analytical Review—A Research Study.* Canada: The Canadian Institute of Chartered Accountants, 1983.

Westwick, C. A. *Do the Figures Make Sense? A Practical Guide to Analytical Review.* England: The Institute of Chartered Accountants in England and Wales, 1981.

9
Modeling Financial and Nonfinancial Relationships Using Regression Analysis

In the previous chapter we discussed using simple reasonableness tests which are nonadvanced mathematical models of financial relationships. One problem with that approach is that the auditor sometimes has difficulty in identifying the form of the model. Another problem is in evaluating exactly what constitutes a significant difference. This chapter extends the previous discussion by explaining the use of a statistical technique for specifying a model called "Regression Analysis." This technique aids the auditor in identifying the appropriate form for a model and in determining what constitutes a significant difference from the model's projection. It is not cost effective unless employed with computer assistance so we will assume that the auditor is using appropriate computer based regression software. The CPA firm of Deloitte Haskins and Sells first introduced computer support for the application of regression analysis in 1971 when it introduced its "STAR" program (Statistical Technique for Analytical Reviews). This system has since been modified and today it is widely used via microcomputers in practice.

A recent national survey of CPAs indicates that they believe regression analysis to be applicable to 16.1% of audits although the estimated frequency of application was only 12% of audits. The corresponding percentages for review engagements were 14.6% and 9.8%, respectively (Daroca and Holder 1985: 88). We believe that these percentages will increase significantly as more auditors become comfortable with the technique, either through academic or other training, and as "user-friendly" microcomputer software makes this technique more cost-effective.

ADVANTAGES OF STATISTICAL MODELING

Two of the problems inherent in analytical auditing are determining (1) what relationship exists between the account being audited and other possible predictive factors and (2) what constitutes a significant difference between the primary result and the projected result. The statistical modeling approaches discussed in this chapter and the following chapter can usually provide either useful information for or solutions for both these problems.

When we consider the first problem of whether there is a significant relationship or pattern in the data, the statistical techniques discussed essentially let the data "speak for itself." This means that the statistical models determine if there is a significant relationship present in the data and advise the auditor of this fact through an appropriate statistical measure. In many circumstances the first attempt at a model may result in no significant relationship or pattern in the data that is useful to the auditor. The techniques determine significance based on objective statistical measures. If there is no statistically significant relationship, the auditor may try to improve the results by trying a different model or by changing the way the model is constructed. For example, the auditor may change the model construction by trying data transformation, lagging some of the variables, adding data periods, and/or adding variables. Alternatively, the auditor may abandon the statistical modeling approach and try some other type of audit test based on an assessment of the costs of modification and the probability of success.

Statistical modeling techniques aid in determining whether a significant difference exists by letting the auditor specify acceptable materiality and risk levels. They then statistically measure if a significant difference exists at risk level specified. The concepts employed in making this analysis are similar to those employed in statistical sampling tests.

BASIC REGRESSION ANALYSIS CONCEPTS

Regression analysis is simply a mathematical approach to describing the relationship between variables. It models the relationship as a linear model. For example, suppose we know that from a company's current sales level of $200,000, every $1 spent on advertising will increase sales by $3. We could express the previous relationship in a mathematical equation as follows:

$$\text{Sales} = \$200,000 + (3 \times \text{Advertising Expenditure})$$

If the company planned to spend $50,000 on advertising then the model would give us a sales prediction of $350,000 as follows:

Sales = $200,000 + (3 × Advertising Expenditure)

Sales = $200,000 + (3 × $50,000)

Sales = $200,000 + ($150,000)

Sales = $350,000

A company might use the model to compute a budgeted sales amount based on budgeted advertising, as in the previous example. An auditor could use budgeted figures but probably would be more interested in using this model to make a projection of what current sales should be based on the amount actually spent on advertising. For example, suppose that an auditor knew that the company's current period sales were actually $374,328 and that the company actually spent $60,000 on advertising in the current period. The model could be used to compute a projected sales amount of $380,000 which could then be compared to actual sales of $374,-328. This would produce a difference of $5,672 which the auditor would have to evaluate for significance:

Sales = $200,000 + (3 × $60,000)

Sales = $200,000 + ($180,000)

Sales = $380,000

Once developed, such models are rather easy to use. The key question for auditors is, How do you develop a Regression Model of this type? The answer is that we estimate such a model from observations of past data values for the variables of interest. In other words, we examine past relationships between the variables and estimate a model from them. To illustrate this suppose that we have the following audited sales and advertising data:

Year	Sales	Advertising
1	$225,000	$7,000
2	$232,000	$10,000
3	$265,000	$27,000
4	$315,000	$34,000
5	$320,000	$39,000

This data is graphed via a scatter diagram in Figure 9.1, Graph of sales and advertising. We can see from the data in the graph that as advertising increases sales increase. In fact, the upward trend in both items appears to be almost a straight line. We can describe a straight line with the following equation

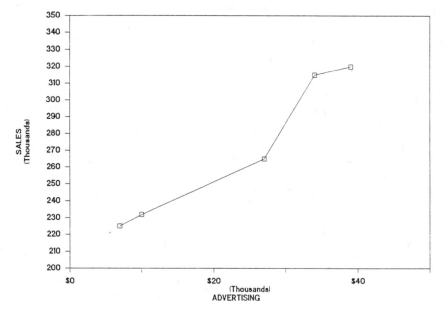

Figure 9.1. Graph of sales and advertising.

$$Y = a + bX$$

where:

Y = dependent variable (sales in our case)
X = independent variable (advertising in our case)
a = constant or fixed term
b = slope of line.

One way to fit a line to the data would be to use a ruler and simply draw the line so that it appears to go through the middle of the data points. This is called "freehand regression" or "eyeball regression" and parallels the graphical method previously discussed in Chapter 4. The problem with this approach is that each auditor comes up with a slightly different line.

We can statistically fit a line to the data points using a method called "Least Squares." This method mathematically minimizes the vertical deviations from the fitted line so as to produce a *single line* that best fits the data points. The least squares computations are mathematically complex so we will not discuss them in detail. Auditors really only need to understand the concept of a mathematically fitted line, not the computations necessary to do so. Computer software will quickly perform these computations. If auditors invest in appropriate computer software, they simply need to be able to understand and appropriately work with the results of the computer processing.

When we use the least squares method to fit a line we obtain estimated or average values for the a and b terms in our linear equation. We use the terms "estimated or average values" because very rarely, would our line exactly fit the underlying data points. The data points would not normally all fall on the fitted line. The fitted line represents our best estimate of the "true" relationship between the variables. We will rarely obtain this "true" relationship because the data will not be perfect and we usually will not know all the factors affecting the "true" relationship. This means that there normally will be some degree of unexplained fluctuation around the regression line. What we are really doing is taking a sample of observations and using it to estimate the true underlying relationship between the variables observed. We know that whenever we sample, we produce an estimated or average value and not the true value for the population. We can only obtain the true value if we 100 percent test the population.

USING ELECTRONIC WORKSHEET SOFTWARE TO PERFORM SIMPLE REGRESSION

In order to further illustrate and explain the previous concepts we will use an electronic worksheet package called LOTUS 1 2 3™ to calculate the regression equation. Table 9.1, Simple Regression via Electronic Worksheet Software, contains a printout of the worksheet containing the previous data on sales and advertising.

Once the data is entered in the worksheet a sequence of three keystrokes (/, D, and R) produces a menu of regression options. The next step is to define the "X-range" which is the advertising data and the "Y-range" which is the sales data. The "Output-Range," where the regression statistics are to be displayed, is then specified. The "Go" command then produces the regression data which is displayed.

The regression equation which was calculated from the five periods of data is slightly different than the Sales = \$200,000 + (3 × Advertising Expense) equation (the "true" relationship which is normally unknown to the auditor) which we first discussed in this chapter. The calculated regression equation is

Sales = \$200,209.20 + 3.042339 (Advertising Expense),

which is expressed in the form of a straight line equation of

TABLE 9.1. Simple Regression via Electronic Worksheet Software.

YEAR	SALES	ADVERTISING
1	225000	7000
2	232000	10000
3	265000	27000
4	315000	34000
5	320000	39000

Regression Output:

Constant	200209.2
Std Err of Y Est	12183.80
R Squared	0.944397
No. of Observations	5
Degrees of Freedom	3

X Coefficient(s) 3.042339
Std Err of Coef. 0.426205

$$Y = a + b(X)$$

The calculated regression equation can be used to make a sales prediction by simply inserting an Advertising Expense amount and summing the equation as previously illustrated.

GOODNESS OF FIT

The least-squares technique of line fitting will fit a linear equation to *any* two sets of data regardless of whether there is any significant relationship between the two variables. An auditor must, therefore, determine if the fitted equation is a good fit. A statistical measure called the "Coefficient of Determination," more commonly R^2, helps determine how good the fitted equation is. The R^2 represents the percentage of explained fluctuation in the data as compared to the total fluctuation in the data. It varies from 0, which means that the equation explained none of the change in the dependent variable, to 1, which means that the equation explains all of the change in the dependent variable. An R^2 of approximately .7 or better is generally deemed acceptable for audit purposes. The R^2 for the equation computed in Table 9.1 was .944397. This means that 94% of the fluctuation in sales was explained by the change in advertising expense and only 6% was unexplained. This would be an extremely good R^2 in an actual audit. We can summarize this discussion into the following practical rule of thumb: *Disregard regression equations that do not produce an R^2 of approximately .70 or better.*

EVALUATION OF STANDARD ERROR

Even though the computed regression equation may fit the data fairly well it still may not be useful for audit purposes if it has a fairly significant error associated with it. A statistical measure called the "Standard Error of the Estimate" helps an auditor to determine how large an error range a particular regression equation has. The error range can be used to compute an amount or limit which would be regarded as a normal fluctuation from the regression line. In a normal analytical auditing regression test, an auditor would define a significant fluctuation as being two times the standard error of the estimate. This would provide the auditor with 95% confidence (only a 5% error chance) that all normal fluctuations would be less than this amount. The auditor would, therefore, conclude that any fluctuations larger than this amount constituted abnormal fluctuations and required investigation by the auditor.

The standard error of the estimate for the regression equation computed in Table 9.1 was $12,183.80. Therefore, we would define a normal fluctuation as being $24,367.60 (2 times $12,183.80). If we assume actual advertising expense for year 6 was $60,000 and actual recorded sales were $374,328 we would make the following computation projecting sales, using a slightly rounded version of the regression equation from Table 9.1:

$$\text{Projected Sales} = \$200,209 + 3.04 \, (\$60,000)$$

$$\text{Projected Sales} = \$382,609.$$

The projected sales figure of $382,609 would then be compared to the recorded sales figure of $374,328 to compute the actual difference of $8,281. Since this is less than $24,367.60 (two times the standard error of the estimate) we would accept the actual sales figure as being a normal fluctuation from the regression equation.

In evaluating the usefulness of an individual regression equation an auditor will have to determine if the normal fluctuation would reasonably correspond to what constitutes a significant difference in the account. For example, suppose an auditor used a materiality rule of thumb and decided that a difference of $15,000 in the sales account would be a significant difference. The normal fluctuation limit of $24,367.60 clearly exceeds this figure so the regression equation would be of reduced evidential value.

One reason the normal fluctuation limit was so large in this example was that we computed the regression equation based on only five data observations thus introducing more uncertainty into our computation of the normal fluctuation limit. In an actual audit we would normally use at least 24 data observations which should produce a much lower normal fluctuation limit. We can summarize this discussion with the following practical rule of thumb: *A regression equation has negligible evidential value if two times the standard error exceeds the materiality limit for the account.* A related practical rule of thumb is: *The regression equation should be developed from 24 or more data observations.*

MULTIPLE REGRESSION

In the previous example we developed a simple regression equation that used only one variable, advertising expense, to predict sales. What if an auditor suspects that there are several possible predictive variables? Can a regression equation use more than one predictive variable? The answer is *yes* and that the auditor must use multiple regression.

Multiple regression is a mathematical technique very similar to simple regression. It employs two or more predictors in a linear model of the following form

$$Y = a + B_1X_1 + B_2X_2 + \ldots + B_nX_n$$

where,

Y = dependent variable (variable to be predicted)
a = constant or fixed term
B_1 = coefficient of first independent variable
X_1 = first independent variable (first predictive variable)
B_2 = coefficient of second independent variable
X_2 = second independent variable (second predictive variable)
B_n = coefficient of last independent variable
X_n = last independent variable where number of independent variables
runs from 1 to n (last predictive variable).

The term "linear" regression model refers to a regression model that is linear in the parameters of the model but not necessarily in the variables employed in the model. In other words, the term linear refers to the coefficients of the model not to the predictive variables employed in the model. For example, the predictive variable X_1 might represent X^3, (X raised to the third power) which is not a linear variable. The coefficient for X_1 which is B_1, however, could not be raised to a power and would be a first order (no exponent) term.

Although the multiple regression equation appears to be much more complicated than a simple regression equation, in fact, it may be only slightly more difficult to use in a computerized environment. The auditor would still input data for selected variables and allow the computer software to fit an equation to the data. The only extra complexity would be in evaluating whether each of the variables in the equation was significant. This chore can be avoided if the auditor uses a type of regression called "stepwise" regression which automatically evaluates each of the potential predictive variables and discards any which are not individually significant. In order to keep this introduction to regression relatively simple, we will use stepwise regression in this chapter to construct a multiple regression equation. In the next chapter we will use nonstepwise regression and explain how the auditor could evaluate the individual variables for significance.

MULTIPLE REGRESSION STEPS

The normal steps in performing a stepwise regression analysis in an audit setting are:

- Determine if application appears cost- beneficial.
- Obtain data for variable of interest and potential predictive variables.
- Input variables into computer file.
- Input or determine materiality criteria.
- Input or determine risk criteria for test.
- Use software to compute regression equation and related statistics.
- Review equation for appropriateness considering R^2 and standard error of the estimate.
- Determine if regression assumptions are appropriately met, if not, consider dropping or adding variables, lagging data, and/or data transformations.
    Normality of errors.
    Autocorrelation of errors.
    Heteroskedasticity of errors.
- Use the regression equation to make forecasts.
- Compare regression forecast with actual result and evaluate difference in terms of statistical standard error of the estimate.

MULTIPLE REGRESSION EXAMPLE

In order to illustrate the concepts of multiple regression let us turn to a realistic example related to audit planning. Assume that an auditor has a client that provides financial services through offices in thirty locations throughout the southeast. A checking account and accounting records are maintained at each operating location under the control of the individual office managers. A monthly summary of operating and financial activity is prepared in a specified format and forwarded to the home office. A significant major expense category is office overhead which include such items as rent, utilities, telephones, copiers, janitorial, and advertising. The auditor would like to construct a multiple regression model that would provide an accurate prediction of what the monthly overhead expense should be for each individual office. Offices with significant differences from the regression projections will be selected for a visit and certain detailed testing.

The auditor has obtained the prior year and current year data for twenty-four of the offices. The remaining offices were opened at some point during the prior year and, therefore, not deemed directly comparable to the older offices. The auditor believes that the following variables are potentially significant predictive variables for Office Overhead Expense—square feet of floor space, age of office building, number of employees, cost of living index for city where office is located, and number of clients served by the office. Table 9.2, Multiple Regression Data, lists this data.

The steps involved in performing the stepwise multiple regression analytical auditing test are:

- Enter the Table 9.2 data in a computer file where it can be accessed by the regression software.
- Compare totals for the computer file to the original data source to make sure that no data has been lost or altered.
- Identify each of the five variables for the regression software.
- Instruct the computer software as to which of the five variables are to be predicted (sales).
- Instruct the computer software as to which of the five variables are to be the predictors (square footage, age of office building, cost of living index, and number of clients).
- Tell the computer software which data points are to be used to construct the regression equation (the 24 data points from the prior year).
- Have the computer software compute the stepwise regression equation.
- Examine the printout to see if there is a problem with any regression assumptions.

TABLE 9.2. Multiple Regression Data.

OFFICE NUMBER	OFFICE OVERHEAD EXPENSE	SQUARE FEET OF FLOOR SPACE	AGE OF OFFICE BUILDING	NUMBER OF EMPLOYEES	COST OF LIVING INDEX	NUMBER OF CLIENTS
PRIOR YEAR						
1	218955	1589	3	15	1.03	2450
2	224513	1912	19	15	1.00	2310
3	66542	741	2	5	0.99	887
4	212349	1839	3	17	0.93	2655
5	161915	1478	14	13	0.98	2213
6	42469	744	11	3	0.99	518
7	55379	790	14	4	0.95	807
8	100955	925	21	8	1.05	1149
9	111487	1364	3	9	1.05	1490
10	117974	1197	7	9	1.01	1559
11	56248	689	6	5	1.06	708
12	64782	742	20	4	0.97	818
13	70893	501	9	5	1.09	943
14	103057	1088	9	9	0.99	1613
15	137049	1268	8	11	0.96	1913
16	136687	1156	19	12	0.96	1888
17	57731	807	19	4	1.04	739
18	160098	1778	15	14	0.92	2134
19	222472	1533	15	14	1.07	2332
20	153061	1686	18	13	0.96	2155
21	171788	1560	8	12	0.95	1879
22	167373	1612	4	12	1.03	2040
23	188435	1812	15	14	1.00	2147
24	35099	607	11	2	0.95	492
CURRENT YEAR						
1	202705	1589	4	15	1.04	2693
2	177178	1912	20	16	1.00	2464
3	71078	741	3	3	1.00	971
4	184870	1839	4	17	0.94	2944
5	198487	1478	15	13	0.98	2611

(*continued*)

TABLE 9.2. (*Continued*)

6	46244	744	12	3	0.98	559
7	56298	790	15	5	0.94	810
8	97222	925	22	8	1.05	1260
9	109829	1364	4	6	1.05	1538
10	107554	1197	8	7	1.01	1764
11	54091	689	7	5	1.06	736
12	59731	742	21	3	0.98	842
13	61025	501	10	2	1.09	899
14	121201	1088	10	7	0.99	1758
15	163783	1268	9	11	0.96	2048
16	161915	1156	20	9	0.96	2057
17	49497	807	20	3	1.04	716
18	149595	1778	16	13	0.93	2423
19	198631	1533	16	14	1.06	2454
20	176763	1686	19	12	0.96	2246
21	152017	1560	9	10	0.95	1846
22	146462	1612	5	10	1.03	2242
23	202638	1812	16	13	1.00	2401
24	27105	607	12	1	0.95	469

- Determine if the coefficient of determination (R^2) is acceptable.
- Determine if the standard error of the estimate is acceptable.
- Have the computer software use the regression equation to make projections for the current period.
- Identify any current period values which deviate by more than two standard errors from their projected value.
- Appropriately followup or investigate any deviations identified.

MULTIPLE REGRESSION EXAMPLE RESULTS

Table 9.3, Multiple Regression Output, illustrates the type of output that microcomputer multiple regression software can produce. It was obtained by regressing the data in Table 9.2 in the manner previously discussed. A close inspection of Table 9.3 reveals the following information:

- A regression equation with only two predictive variables was obtained. The other two predictive variables were deemed not significant by the stepwise multiple regression software.
- The regression equation is of the form: Office Overhead = −36,207 + (5237 × Age of Building) + (19799 × Number of Employees).

TABLE 9.3. Multiple Regression Output.

STEPWISE MULTIPLE REGRESSION MODEL

DESCRIPTION	INPUT DATA		REGRESSION FUNCTION ETC.	
	MEAN	STANDARD ERROR	CONSTANT OR COEFFICIENT	STANDARD ERROR
CONSTANT			-36206.5200	
INDEPENDENT VARIABLES				
X2 AGE OF BLDG	11.3750	6.1631	5236.7539	2541.3701
X3 NUM EMPLOYEES	9.5417	4.5490	19799.4902	3443.0720
DEPENDENT VARIABLE				
Y OFFICE OVERHEAD	212281.7030	118551.7030		
Y' REGRESSION ESTIMATE			212281.7030	75050.3830
COEFFICIENT OF :				
CORRELATION			0.7963	
REGRESSION IMPROVEMENT			0.3669	
RESIDUAL VARIATION			0.3535	

REGRESSION ESTIMATE [Y'(t)] OF OFFICE OVERHEAD FOR OBSERVATION t :
$Y'(t) = -36206.52 + 5236.754*X2(t) + 19799.49*X3(t)$

- All regression assumptions are acceptably met according to a message from the stepwise regression software.
- The coefficient of determination (R^2) is .63 which is a bit low for normal audit purposes since .70 or higher is our rule of thumb. We can use an R^2 of that value but the evidence produced will be weaker.
- The standard error of the estimate is $75,050. Two times this standard error, or $150,100, would be the amount that we would use in deciding if deviations from the regression projection were acceptable or not. Since the total overhead for the current year is $5,128,173 the average overhead per location is $213,674 ($5,128,173/24). The deviation limit of $150,100 is clearly too large to be useful since it is such a large percentage (70%) of the average overhead per location of $213,674. Also, the deviation limit is 2.9% of the overall account total ($150,100/$5,128,173 = 2.9%) while 1% or less would be more appropriate for a monthly test of this type.
- Although the standard error is too large to be useful we will go ahead and use it to identify unusual fluctuations simply to illustrate the process. Table 9.4, Identification of Unusual Fluctuations, illustrates the computations involved. As seen in Table 9.4, only location 9 has a regression projection which deviates from the book amount by more than $150,100.
- We would now be required either to investigate or increase audit testing for location 9 since it had a significant difference from the regression projection.

An appropriate question is what should an auditor do when encountering a low R^2 and/or a high standard error as in the previous example? There are three basic possibilities that we will discuss in the order they should be considered by an auditor:

1. Consider transforming one or more of the predictive variables in order to raise the R^2 or lower the standard error.
2. Seek additional predictive variables which were not used in the original equation. Rerun the data using these additional variables to see if that will raise the R^2 or lower the standard error.
3. Abandon any further work on the regression test. Include it in working papers but note that due to the problems previously discussed it only provides weak evidence for the overhead account balance.

If the auditor very carefully planned the analytical auditing test then options (1) and (2) would have been previously considered. The auditor would probably then go straight to option (3).

TABLE 9.4. Identification of Unusual Fluctuations.

Store location	Book value of office overhead	Regression estimate of office overhead*	Difference between book value and regression estimate	Two times standard error of $ 75,050	Difference exceeding two times the standard error**
1	$ 180,713	$281,733	$ -101,020	$150,100	
2	392,675	385,320	7,355	150,100	
3	141,086	38,902	102,184	150,100	
4	249,417	321,332	-71,915	150,100	
5	447,688	299,738	147,950	150,100	
6	107,908	86,033	21,875	150,100	
7	60,809	141,342	-80,533	150,100	
8	183,826	237,398	-53,572	150,100	
9	276,994	103,537	173,457	150,100	$ 23,457
10	145,146	144,284	862	150,100	
11	123,407	99,448	23,959	150,100	
12	75,739	133,164	-57,425	150,100	
13	106,569	55,760	50,809	150,000	
14	117,003	154,758	-37,754	150,100	
15	282,807	228,719	54,088	150,100	
16	348,061	246,724	101,337	150,100	
17	128,365	127,927	438	150,100	
18	215,140	304,975	-89,835	150,100	
19	469,216	324,774	144,442	150,100	
20	289,586	300,886	-11,300	150,100	
21	195,226	208,919	-13,693	150,100	
22	162,831	187,972	-25,141	150,100	
23	378,592	304,975	73,617	150,100	
24	49,369	46,434	2,935	150,100	
Totals	$5,128,173	$4,765,053	$363,120		

* The regression estimate is obtained by substituting current year values for age of building and number of employees in the following equation:

Office overhead = -36,207 + (5,237 * Age of building) + (19799 * Number of employees)

** Two times the standard error roughly corresponds to a 95% confidence interval. Therefore, there is less than a 5% probability that the book value for store location 9 could be correct based on the regression equation.

REGRESSION ASSUMPTIONS

Regression analysis depends upon three basic assumptions about errors. By errors we mean the differences between the recorded values and the regression projections or estimates of the recorded values. These errors are sometimes also called residuals. The three basic assumptions are: (1) the errors are normally distributed, (2) the errors are not autocorrelated, and (3) the errors do not display heteroskedasticity.

The first assumption, normality of errors, simply means that the errors, are normally distributed around the regression line. This would occur when they form a bell-shaped normal curve pattern. This assumption may be easily statistically tested using the chi-square statistic.

The second assumption, lack of autocorrelation, means that the individual errors are not related to past errors. This would occur when individual errors move randomly and not in any particular pattern with respect to past errors. This assumption may be easily statistically tested using the Durbin-Watson statistic.

The third assumption, heteroskedasticity of errors, means that the errors are distributed in the same manner through all the observation periods and not bunched more tightly in one observation period than in another. This assumption may be easily statistically evaluated using Bartlett's chi-square.

The most cost-effective regression software automatically checks the previous assumptions and prints out an error message to the auditor if a problem exists. This means that the auditor only has to be concerned with these assumptions on an exception basis. The software used for the previous example operated in this manner. We will discuss these assumptions in more depth in the latter part of the next chapter when we go through another example using software which does not check these assumptions automatically.

MULTICOLLINEARITY IN MULTIPLE-REGRESSION

Another potential problem in multiple regression, although not actually an error, is multicollinearity. This means that one predictive variable is related to another predictive variable. This condition causes the computed R^2 of the multiple-regresssion equation to be overstated. The R^2 of the equation will then appear to be better that the actual predictive power of the underlying equation warrants. The solution to this problem is to drop one of the related variables from the equation. Stepwise regression automatically does this thus eliminating a potential problem for the auditor. Nonstepwise regression software is used in the example in the latter part of the next chapter so we will have an opportunity to see how an auditor could handle this problem with regular regression software.

An alternative approach is to use a modified regression technique called "Ridge-regression Analysis." Discussion of this technique is beyond the scope of this book but information may be found in many advanced statistical analysis texts.

REFERENCES

Albrecht, W. S. "Analytical Reviews for Internal Auditors," *The Internal Auditor* (August 1980): 20-25.

Daroca, F. P., and W. W. Holder. "The Use of Analytical Procedures in Review and Audit Engagement," *Auditing: Journal of Practice & Theory* (Spring 1985): 80-92.

Deloitte Haskins & Sells. *STAR Program Reference Manual.* New York: Deloitte Haskins & Sells, 1986.

Dillon, W. R., and M. Goldstein. *Multivariate Analysis—Methods and Applications.* New York: John Wiley & Sons, Inc., 1984.

Ferris, K. R., and K. L. Tennant. "New Tools for Analytical Reviews," *The Internal Auditor* (December 1982): 14-17.

Fox, J. *Linear Statistical Models and Related Methods.* New York: John Wiley & Sons, Inc., 1984.

Kenny, D. A. *Correlation and Causality.* New York: John Wiley & Sons, Inc., 1979.

Willis, R. E., and N. L. Chervany. *Statistical Analysis and Modeling for Management Decision-Making.* Belmont, California: Wadsworth Publishing Company, Inc., 1974.

10
Statistical Modeling of Time-series Trends

In Chapter 4 we discussed basic concepts about time-series and reviewed five simple trend analysis techniques. This chapter extends that discussion about time-series concepts. It then explains and illustrates two statistical techniques for performing time-series analysis, the ARIMA model and structural regression analysis. These techniques are not cost-effective unless implemented with computer assistance so auditors wishing to implement these techniques are advised to acquire microcomputer software that is commercially available for implementing these techniques.

TIME-SERIES CONCEPTS

Time-series analysis is a search for patterns in past data of a particular variable so that those patterns can be used to predict current or future period values of the variable. When a variable's patterns in past data are appropriately identified then these patterns and the variable are mathematically modeled. The mathematical model is then used to make a forecast for the variable. This approach makes the extremely important assumption that the past patterns (relationships) represented in the model will continue into the foreseeable future. This assumption may not be appropriate if underlying economic conditions change in some significant fashion.

The most successful approach to identification of patterns in time-series data is called time-series decomposition (component analysis). It involves decomposing (breaking down) the past data using somewhat standard models in order to identify the patterns. As the individual patterns are identified they are each mathematically modeled and their effects are removed from the data so that the search for additional patterns can continue. When all patterns that can be identified are removed from the data the residual remains is assumed to be random (unpatterned) data. This random (unpatterned) data component represents the amount of forecasting error remaining in the data. If it is relatively large, the use of a time-series modeling approach may have to be abandoned by the auditor. Once a time-series has been decomposed into its underlying patterns, each of which have been modeled, the individual models can be aggregated to form an overall model of the time-series variable. This overall model is then used to make projections.

The search for underlying patterns can usually proceed in a systematic fashion since statisticians have observed certain types of patterns regularly recurring in many different time-series. Three very common underlying patterns are the time-series trend pattern, seasonal patterns, and cyclical patterns.

The time-series trend pattern is the long-run tendency of the data either to increase or decrease over time. For example, if we examined the sales of a company which had gradually increased from $4,565,987 in 1970 to $66,213,344 in 1988 we would say that the long-run trend was to increase. Using the average change method discussed in Chapter 4 we can calculate that the specific trend was an average of a +79% sales growth per year.

The seasonal pattern is one that recurs over a specific time interval within a year. For example, if we are analyzing the sales of a company and find that it experiences a large sales increase every November and December, due to Christmas, that would be seasonal pattern. A seasonal pattern can occur more frequently than once a year and may occur over any standard time interval, such as quarterly. An example of a quarterly seasonal pattern would be a company that grants customers a discount on cumulative purchases that exceed some standard level within each calendar quarter. If customers usually buy more during the last month of every quarter in order to take advantage of the discount then the company may experience a sales increase during the last month of every quarter, a type of seasonal pattern.

A cyclical pattern is a pattern that reoccurs over some longer interval than a year. For example, suppose a company sold building materials. If it experienced a sales downturn periodically whenever the general economy went into a recession, which historically has happened every four to six years, then sales would follow a cyclical pattern. A cyclical pattern is somewhat similar to a seasonal pattern in that it reoccurs at a regular interval except that the interval exceeds one year in length.

When the effects of the three standard patterns are removed from the time-series the data that remains, "residuals," may or may not contain additional patterns. An auditor would examine these "residuals" to see if any additional patterns remained. For example, an auditor may note from the residuals that three sharp downturns in sales have occurred over the last fifteen years. Investigation may reveal that these sales decreases resulted from strikes that halted production. The auditor may also determine that these strikes only occurred when a union contract expired. Contract expirations may have been at irregular intervals due to different length contracts being negotiated in the past. The strike effect could then be removed from the data. In order to make a projection the auditor would determine whether the union contract would be expiring during the projection period. If this were expected to happen then the forecast should reflect a strike effect.

After removing the strike effect from the past data, the auditor would then examine the remaining residuals. If there were no further patterns apparent, these residuals would be regarded as a random factor which will influence the accuracy of future forecasts. Obviously if the patterns identified caused most of the fluctuation in the time-series, thereby leaving relatively small residuals, forecasts should be fairly accurate. On the other hand, if the identified patterns only caused a moderate amount of the fluctuation in the time-series, thereby leaving relatively large residuals, the related forecasts would not be very accurate. The average value and dispersion of the residuals may be statistically measured thus aiding the auditor in determining how strong, statistically speaking, the model of the time-series was.

We can algebraically model a time-series with trend, cyclical, and seasonal patterns as follows

$$F = T \times C \times S \times I$$

where,

F = Time-series value
T = Trend component
C = Cyclical component
S = Seasonal component
I = Irregular component (residual component)

As individual components are identified they can be used to restructure the equation to help isolate remaining components.

Since a mathematical decomposition of a time-series would be too complex for this book, we will illustrate the process in a graphical manner. Figure 10.1, Sales time-series, displays a sales time-series for a sixty month period. This time-series was artificially created in order to easily illustrate the various components of a typical time-series.

A trend component is evident from the upward slope in the overall

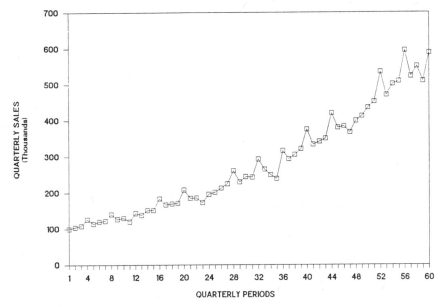

Figure 10.1. Sales time-series.

time-series. The trend component has been isolated and is more clearly displayed in Figure 10.2, Sales time-series—trend component.

Once the trend component is removed from the time-series, the cyclical component is more clearly evident. Approximately every twelve quarters there is a slight downturn in the overall time-series which lasts for three quarters. This component is displayed in Figure 10.3, Sales time-series—cyclical component.

A seasonal component is also present in the time-series. Sales decreases slightly every fourth quarter. The seasonal component is displayed in Figure 10.4, Sales time-series—seasonal component.

The residual component reflects the data that is left in the sales time-series after the three previous patterns are mathematically removed from the overall time-series. It is displayed in Figure 10.5, Sales time-series—residual component.

NAIVE VERSUS STRUCTURAL TIME-SERIES MODELS

When they use only data in an individual time-series trend to model a time-series (make projections), both univariate and multivariate models are essentially descriptive in nature since they do not attempt to model the underlying causal relationship. They only model the information the

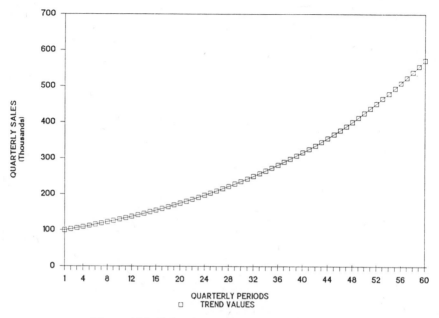

Figure 10.2. Sales time-series—trend component.

auditor is able to observe in the time-series data. Forecasters call these time-series models "naive" because they ignore the underlying factors causing the change in the time-series. Naive time-series models can be quite good if the underlying conditions persist for considerable periods of time. When the underlying conditions change, however, naive time-series models can make very inaccurate projections. Thus, by their basic nature they are inherently short-range. The farther into the future they are used to project, the riskier their projections become since the chance for a change in underlying conditions increases. Accordingly, auditors should use these models for only relatively short forecasts probably not exceeding a year in length.

Structural time-series models attempt to make predictions based on a model of the causal factors underlying a particular economic variable. Ideally the causal factors should be based on underlying economic theory. If economic theory with respect to a particular variable is not developed, incomplete, or ambiguous, then the auditor may have to determine the appropriate predictive variables using only general economic theory as guidance. Structural time-series models would be generally preferred whenever an auditor either has a strong basis for identifying the causal relationships or has to make a long-run projection.

If two different modeling approaches are tried and equally powerful

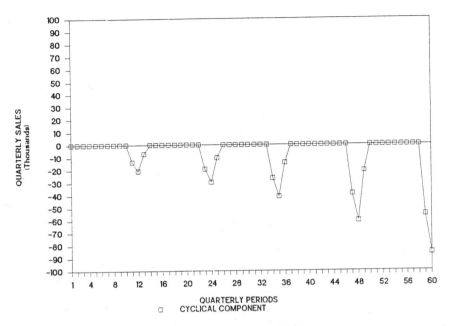

Figure 10.3. Sales time-series—cyclical component.

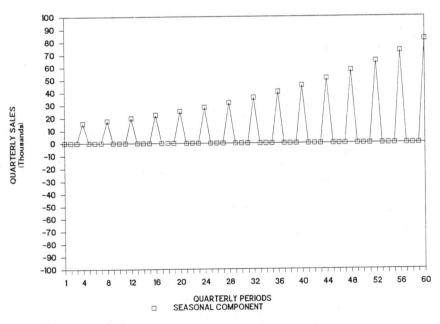

Figure 10.4. Sales time-series—seasonal component.

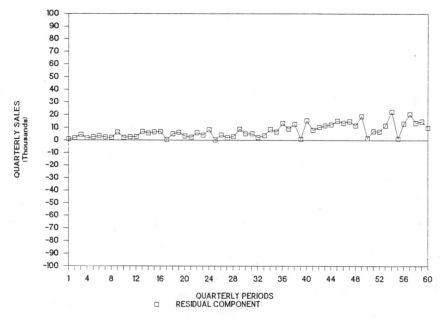

Figure 10.5. Sales time-series—residual component.

models are developed, then the auditor should use the principle of *Occam's Razor* and select the simpler model. William of Occam (1300-1349) was an English philosopher who proposed the widely accepted rule that when we have two equivalent explanations (models) for the same phenomenon that we should accept the simpler explanation.

The remainder of this chapter will be devoted to an explanation and illustration of a naive forecasting approach to time-series trends called ARIMA Time-series Modeling and to a structural forecasting approach to time-series trends called Structural Regression Time-series Modeling.

ARIMA TIME-SERIES MODELS

One type of model that has been very successful in forecasting time-series trends is the auto-regressive integrative moving average (ARIMA) model which is actually a combination of three separate univariate models, the auto-regressive, the integrative, and the moving average. The ARIMA modeling approach is sometimes called Box-Jenkins Time-series Modeling after two individuals whose research helped advance this type of modeling (Box and Jenkins 1976).

The ARIMA modeling approach is not currently used by many auditors. In fact, a recent national survey indicates that CPAs believe that ARIMA is applicable to only 9% of audit engagements and is applied in only 3.4% of audit engagements. Percentages were similar for review engagements (Daroca and Holder 1985: 88). Why then, you might ask, is ARIMA included in this book? The answer to this question can be found in the following comment:

Arrington and Hillison [1982] analyzed the statistical effectiveness of limited trend models, regression analysis, and time series models (ARIMA) in the analytical review process. They concluded that ARIMA is theoretically the most effective analytical review technique. However, "due to extensive data requirements, the complex notational appearance, difficulty with the ability to interpret, and the direct and indirect cost of operationalizing, the ARIMA modeling process may be limited in terms of current application by auditors (Arrington and Hillison 1982: 48)."

(Dugan, Gentry and Shriver 1985: 11-12)

Dugan, Gentry and Shriver then go on to propose a modeling approach similar to ARIMA called the X-11 Model which was developed by the U.S. Bureau of Census. They believe that the X-11 Model overcomes some of the problems associated with the ARIMA modeling approach. They note that the X-11 Model is commercially available for microcomputer use. We believe that the operational difficulties of using the ARIMA approach will be minimized with "user-friendly" software and that use of this approach or new versions of it will increase in auditing.

The ARIMA model actually is not a single model. Rather it is more of a systematic approach to studying a time-series that consists of an orderly consideration of a number of standard models until the model (or models) that best describe the data series are identified. This technique is reasonably complicated and a complete coverage of the technique is not possible in this book. Since we are assuming computer support for this technique and the better computer packages go through this analysis, more or less, on an automatic basis, it is probably not necessary for an auditor to know all the technical details of the this approach if high quality software will be used. Accordingly, our coverage in this chapter will be limited to a review of the basic ARIMA approach.

One limitation of the ARIMA modeling approach is that a minimum of 50 periods of data are needed to appropriately identify the model parameters. This means that yearly data will not be appropriate for this type of modeling.

The ARIMA approach can be best understood as a series of logical steps based on the previously discussed concept of orderly time-series decomposition. An approach to accomplishing this is to:

1. Plot the time-series data on a graph.
2. Examine the data plot for possible errors or outliers (extreme data values). Correct any errors. Determine reason for outliers and consider removing them from data series if they are deemed nontypical data values (e.g., not expected to reoccur).
3. Examine the data plot for possible structural change. If a major structural change in the time-series has occurred, determine the cause (e.g., oil embargo, merger, introduction of new product line). Give consideration to dropping the pre-structural change portion of the time-series from the analysis and only continuing the analysis with the post-structural change data.
4. Examine the data plot for an underlying trend. If a trend exists remove it from the time-series by using a likely ARIMA model. The statistical modeling approach of first differences is the generally preferred approach to trend removal. First differences is a technique to remove trend by converting the time-series data to the difference between each data value and its preceding data value. If an examination of a data plot of the first differences indicates that it did not effectively remove the trend, use another data transformation modeling approach such as a conversion to logarithms (discussed in Chapter 4) to remove the trend.
5. Fit several likely ARIMA models which would be appropriate to model seasonal and cyclical movements to the de-trended data and compute their autocorrelations for each time period. The autocorrelation is a statistical measure of the strength of the relationship of a variable and a lagged value of the same variable (how much each time-series data item is statistically related to its own preceding value).
6. For each model fitted in the preceding step, compare its computed autocorrelations with its theoretical autocorrelation for the same time period. From the field of likely models fitted in the previous step, select the model or models whose computed autocorrelations for each time period appear to reasonably approximate their theoretical autocorrelations for the corresponding time periods.
7. Compute the model equations for the possible models identified in the step 6. The model equations are the mathematical formulations of the models as applied to the specific time-series.
8. Perform the following statistical tests on the model or models computed in step 7: (a) statistical test to determine if the model coefficients (values) are significant, and (b) statistical test to see if, after use of the model on the time-series, the remaining residuals do not exhibit any significant pattern. Drop from consideration any model which fails these statistical tests.
9. If more than one model remains after performing the previous statistical tests, judgmentally select the best model after consideration of all

model characteristics. (If no model passes the tests in step 8 consider some non-ARIMA type of time-series forecasting such as a structural regression time-series model.)

10. Make a projection using the ARIMA model determined in the step 9.

STRUCTURAL REGRESSION TIME-SERIES MODELING

The mechanics of regression analysis were explained in Chapter 9 so we will focus here on the use of the technique in time- series modeling. A regression model is frequently one of the ARIMA models which is fitted during the decomposition of a time-series. That type of use, however, is a naive use since the regression variable used to make the prediction is time. In this section we will focus on the use of structural regression which involves using predictive variables which are thought either to cause or be theoretically related to the time-series variable which is of interest.

One problem confronting an auditor using structural regression in time-series modeling is, What predictive variables (independent variables) should be used to predict changes in the time-series data? This question is really an extension of the same question that we faced in Chapter 8 when we tried to determine appropriate simple reasonableness tests. In fact, many of the relationships that we might model through simple reasonableness tests can also be modeled with regression analysis.

Potential independent variables can usually be classified into three distinct groups. The group classification for an individual variable might be different for clients in different lines of business. The three groups are:

1. Known predictors. This would include all variables that an auditor would know, either from economic theory or past experience with the client, are related to the time-series item that the auditor is trying to predict. For example, assume the time-series variable we are trying to predict is sales. An auditor might know from economic theory that the rate of inflation would be one of the factors influencing sales.
2. Promising predictors. This would include variables for which the auditor has some evidence to support a relationship to the time-series item but not enough evidence (e.g., incomplete economic theory) to know with reasonable certainty. For example, if we again assume the time-series variable we are trying to predict is sales, an auditor might believe that past advertising expenditures will have an effect on current period sales.
3. Possible predictors. These are variables that could be predictors but the auditor has no real basis for knowing this. This would usually include all other financial data, operating data, and economic data that was not

included in the previous two categories. For example, the death rate for the overall population might be related to past changes in sales but this would not appear to be either a known or promising predictor for a retail sales store. On the other hand, if we were trying to predict sales for a manufacturer of coffins the same variable would probably fall in either the known or promising predictor category.

An auditor should start with variables from the first group and only move to the second or third groups if an appropriate model cannot be constructed from the first group. The reason for this approach is that our objective is to construct a model of variables that cause the change in the time-series variable we are trying to predict. In time-series data many variables that could be individually significant predictive variables are likely to be highly correlated with each other (move in the same direction) as well as the time-series variable we are trying to predict. This produces the undesirable condition known as multicollinearily into the regression model. Using a classic example, suppose that an auditor used church attendance and liquor consumption as possible predictors of sales for a manufacturer of home appliances. If we applied regression analysis to construct a mathematical model in order to forecast sales, both variables might statistically appear to offer significant predictive power in predicting sales. However, neither appear to have any theoretical basis for being possible predictors of sales for a manufacturer of home appliances. The answer is that both church attendance and liquor consumption are related (correlated) to the general growth in the overall population which, of course, should be the predictor variable used to predict sales. Population growth should fall in either the known or promising variable categories. The other two variables should not be used or only be used with great care since they are not causally related.

Another significant problem faced by the auditor is, What model form is most appropriate? This problem is particularly difficult since there are many different types of regression analysis and many different ways of constructing individual regression models. Cost-effective use of regression analysis in auditing cannot be accomplished in the majority of audits if the auditor has to spend a great deal of time trying to find the right model. Accordingly, we believe and recommend that the only cost-effective approach is to use a computer software package that will answer this question for the auditor. The better software packages typically can conduct a "tournament" where they automatically try various data transformations and pit various models against each other to determine which model provides the best predictions, thus automatically answering the question for the auditor. The exception to this general belief and recommendation would be in a very large audit where the time an individual auditor might spend in searching for an appropriate model could provide a cost-effective payback given the time it might take to obtain assurance about the account from alternative audit tests.

STEPS IN APPLYING REGRESSION ANALYSIS TO TIME-SERIES DATA

An auditor would normally perform each of the following steps in applying regression analysis to time- series data unless using software which automatically performs some of them:

1. Input appropriate variables into computer file.
2. Compute regression equation and related statistics.
3. Evaluate R^2 and F statistics.
4. Examine correlation coefficients for multicollinearity.
5. Evaluate T statistic for each independent variable.
6. Determine if regression assumptions are met.
   A. Normality of errors.
   B. Autocorrelation of errors.
   C. Heteroskedasticity of errors.
7. Use regression equation to make forecast.
8. Compare regression forecast with actual result and evaluate difference in terms of statistical standard error.

EXAMPLE OF STRUCTURAL REGRESSION APPLIED TO TIME-SERIES DATA

In order to illustrate the application of structural regression to time-series data we are going to assume that we want to predict XYZ Company sales revenue for the current year from Product M and believe that advertising expenditures, rate of inflation, prior period sales, and the sales price of a substitute product are promising predictors. We will analyze this data on a step-by-step basis in order to illustrate the steps involved even though the best computer packages will perform all these steps automatically for the auditor.

Step 1. The first step is to gather data on each of these items and input the data into a computer file. We determine that 36 months of data is available for each selected variable which includes the current year under audit. We are assuming that the two prior year's have been audited which means that both Product M sales and advertising expenditures have been audited for periods 1 to 24. We can also assume that the data on rate of inflation and sales price of substitute were taken from industry trade journals. The four variables, therefore, do not need to have any audit procedures applied to them before using. The auditor should consider applying some type of verification procedure to insure its accuracy of any variables produced by the client's information system which had not been previously audited, This data is then entered in a computer file. Table 10.1, Product M Sales and Related Data, is a printout of what we entered in a computer file.

Step 2. The next step is to have the computer software compute a possible regression equation using all four variables. The sales data for months 1 to 24 will be identified as the dependent variable (the variable we want to predict). Advertising expense, inflation rate, and sales price of substitute product for months 1 to 24 will be identified as the independent variables (possible predictors). That means that the latter three variables will be used to try to predict the change in Product M sales. When the data is entered and identified in this manner the computer will calculate a regression equation and related statistics in a few seconds. These items can usually then be examined via a screen display and/or a printout.

Step 3. We would then analyze this computer produced data to see if a significant equation was developed. The two statistical measures to determine the significance of the overall equation are the R^2 statistic and the F statistic. A computer printout indicates the R^2 statistic is .71 and the F statistic is 16 for the computed regression equation. The R^2 statistic indicates the percentage of variation in the independent variable (sales) that the predictive variables can explain. An R^2 of approximately .70 or better is usually deemed acceptable for audit purposes. The F statistic is an overall test of the regression model's significance. An F table gives us an F statistic of 3.1 with a 95 percent confidence level when 3 and 20 degrees of freedom exist. Since our computed model's F statistic of 16 greatly exceeds 3.1 we can conclude that the model is significant.

Step 4. Since we now know that the equation developed is significant, we must check to see if any of the independent variables are significantly enough correlated with each other to produce a multicollinearity problem. We can make this check by examining a printout of correlation coefficients. Using a rule of thumb we would identify as significantly correlated with each other, all independent variables whose correlations *exceed the value produced when the number 2 is divided by the square root of the number of time periods.* In our example this would be the value produced when 2 is divided by the square root of 24. This value is .41. An examination of the correlation coefficients for our independent variables reveals that advertising expenditures and sales price of substitute product are correlated at a .66 level. Since .66 exceeds our rule of thumb amount of .41 this means we have a multicollinearity problem. We can fix this problem by dropping one of the two variables from the equation but the question is which one? The answer to this question may be found by dropping one of the two highly correlated variables (say advertising expenditures) from the equation and rerunning the data a second time using the remaining

TABLE 10.1. Product M Sales and Related Data.

MONTH	PRODUCT M SALES	ADVERTISING EXPENDITURES	RATE OF INFLATION IN %	SALES PRICE OF SUBSTITUTE
1	211854	4500	0.50	10.50
2	225839	4500	0.52	10.50
3	224391	4500	0.56	10.50
4	226862	4500	0.52	10.50
5	232211	4500	0.54	10.50
6	237134	4500	0.53	10.50
7	226896	6000	0.54	10.50
8	239727	6000	0.59	10.50
9	239765	6500	0.58	10.50
10	230910	6500	0.59	10.50
11	231759	6500	0.55	10.50
12	231365	6500	0.50	10.50
13	248070	6700	0.57	11.00
14	240398	6700	0.60	11.00
15	241224	6700	0.52	11.00
16	245320	7000	0.60	11.00
17	247315	7000	0.52	11.00
18	243196	7000	0.50	11.00
19	245059	6000	0.54	11.00
20	257139	6000	0.57	11.00
21	252381	6000	0.59	11.00
22	254352	7000	0.59	11.00
23	260199	7000	0.52	11.00
24	258083	7000	0.51	11.00
25	248109	8000	0.54	11.50
26	250704	8000	0.56	11.50
27	251648	8000	0.56	11.50
28	270087	8000	0.54	11.50
29	255827	8000	0.57	11.50
30	266466	8000	0.54	11.50
31	274625	10000	0.56	11.70
32	271975	10000	0.51	11.70
33	261122	10000	0.53	11.70
34	260059	10000	0.54	11.70
35	277965	10000	0.55	11.70
36	276916	10000	0.59	11.70

variables. The dropped variable (advertising expenditures) would then be included while the other variable (sales price of a substitute product) is dropped and the data is rerun a third time. The F statistic can then be examined for these two subsequent equations and the equation producing the highest F statistic is used, thus dropping the variable that was excluded from that equation. In effect, the highly correlated variable that contributes the least to the F statistic is dropped. When we perform this process for our case, advertising expenditures are dropped and we are left with an equation where the inflation rate and sales price of a substitute product are used to predict sales. An examination of the revised R^2 and F statistic indicate that we still have an equation that may be strong enough to use.

Step 5. We will now examine the T statistic for each of the remaining independent variables to see if they are individually significant. The T statistic measures the significance of each individual variable. A T statistic table tells us that the T statistic for our variables should exceed 1.72 with 21 degrees of freedom and a 95 percent confidence level. Since the computer printout reveals the computed T statistics of the two variables now remaining in the equation, (rate of inflation and sales price of substitute product), each exceed 1.72, both of them remain in the final equation.

Step 6. The next step is to test to see if various regression assumptions are appropriately met. We would normally test the three assumptions, normality of errors, autocorrelation, and heteroskedasticity. These were briefly discussed in the preceding chapter.

The normality of errors may be judgmentally tested by viewing a graph of the error distribution to see if the individual errors appear to follow a normal curve pattern. Alternatively, the auditor may use a chi-square statistic to make this test. If the computed chi-square from the error term is close to zero then the auditor may conclude that the errors are normally distributed. In our example, the computed chi-square statistic was 0.75 which was close enough to zero to indicate that the error distribution is approximately normal.

The autocorrelation of error may be tested with the Durbin-Watson statistic. If the computed Durbin-Watson statistic is in the range from 1 to 3 we would normally assume that the error terms are not significantly autocorrelated. Also, an exact statistical test can be performed using a Durbin-Watson D Statistic table. In our example the computed Durbin-Watson statistic of 1.38 is in the safe range of 1 to 3. It is also less than the critical Durbin-Watson statistic of 2.46 with 20 degrees of freedom and 95% confidence (determined from a Durbin-Watson D Statistic table), so we can conclude that autocorrelation does not exist.

The heteroskedasticity of errors can be evaluated by determining how close Bartlett's chi-square is to zero, the ideal value. Our sample Bartlett's chi-square was 0.22 which indicates no problem with heteroskedasticity of errors.

Step 7. We are now ready to use our regression model to forecast values for the current period. This process is reasonably straightforward. We simply take our final regression equation and substitute in it the independent variable values for the period we want to forecast. The equation can then be algebraically summed to produce the forecast value. The final equation derived from our example data was:

$$\text{Sales} = -188369 + (108843 \times \text{Rate of Inflation})$$
$$+ (34275 \times \text{Sales Price of Substitute Product})$$

Substitute the data values for month 25 to obtain the following forecast:

$$\text{Sales} = -188369 + (108843 \times .56) + (34275 \times 11.50)$$
$$\text{Sales} = 266745$$

Step 8. The final step is to compare the regression forecast of $266,745 with the recorded sales of $263,181 for the same time period and determine whether the difference of $3,564 is statistically significant. We would normally conclude, at a 95% level of confidence, that if the difference is less than two times the standard error of the estimate (a statistic computed by the regression software) the difference is not statistically significant. For our example, the standard error was $7,959 so we would conclude that the difference of $3,564 was not statistically significant ($3,564 is less than 2 times $7,959). An auditor, however, must also evaluate the standard error of the estimate in terms of materiality (or tolerable error) for the account. If two times the standard error exceeds an amount the auditor deems material then the regression test would be limited evidential value. If we use 1% of annual sales amount, a rule of thumb for revenue accounts tested on a monthly basis, as the maximum error we would accept for the account then we can conclude that the standard error is acceptably small since the $15,918 (2 times the standard error of $7,959) is less than $31,706 (1% of $3,170,566, the recorded sales amount for the year).

We could use the previous technique to make a forecast for each month of the current year and evaluate whether any month's sales are statistically significantly different from their forecasted values. Those months that were significantly different could then be selected for other nonanalytical audit tests.

COMPUTER PACKAGES TO FACILITATE TIME-SERIES MODELING

There are many computer software packages available to facilitate time-series modeling and regression analysis. Differences in auditor academic training, experience, computer hardware, and intended usage make it impossible to recommend a package as being "best." Auditors wishing to acquire a package should first identify their expected usage requirements and then review a current article summarizing features of popular packages. Articles may be found in a wide variety of magazines ranging from accounting and auditing journals to specialized computer magazines. For example, see pages 211 to 234 in the August, 1986, issue of *PC Magazine* for an article titled, "Business Forecasting—16 Ways to Predict the Future" which reviewed, evaluated, and made recommendations for sixteen commercially available software packages.

We recommend that auditors make a "hands-on" test of the software before purchasing it. This will help insure that the software will be appropriate for the audit practice for which it is selected. It is important to remember that the biggest cost incurred is usually not the software but the training time invested. The cost of correcting an erroneous selection decision is usually much larger than the mere cost of replacing the software with an alternative package. If the audit practice does not have any professional employees with appropriate background for guiding the selection process then services of a qualified consultant in this area should be sought.

SUMMARY

These comments reflect what the author believes to be the most important points in this book.

The use of analytical auditing has significantly increased in the past two decades as auditors have adopted better techniques and approaches for producing appropriate audit evidence. The search for more efficient and effective ways to conduct an audit coupled with changes in available technology will continue to produce an increase in the use analytical auditing.

Traditional analytical auditing techniques are continually evolving and improving. New techniques are being developed and implemented. Auditors must keep pace with these changes or risk having their skills become obsolete.

Developments in technology, techniques, and evidence theory are producing a more objective approach to many audit decisions. This book has reviewed both current developments and analytical auditing techniques in an effort to help auditors bridge the gap between the past and the future.

The author finds continuing relevance in a quote which has been attributed to John Wooden, a legendary basketball coach: "It's what you learn after you know it all that counts" (Peter 1977: 279).

REFERENCES

Arrington, C. E., W. Hillison, and R. C. Icerman, "Research In Analytical Review: The State of The Art." *Journal of Accounting Literature* (1983): 151–185.

Box, G. E. P., and G. Jenkins, *Time Series Analysis, Forecasting, and Control,* rev. ed., San Francisco, California: Holden-Day, 1976.

Daroca, F. P., and W. W. Holder. "The Use of Analytical Procedures in Review and Audit Engagements," *Auditing: A Journal of Practice & Theory* (Spring 1985): 80–92.

Dillon, W. R., and M. Goldstein. *Multivariate Analysis—Methods and Applications.* New York: John Wiley & Sons, 1984.

Doane, D. P. *Exploring Statistics with the IBM P.C.* Reading, Massachusetts, Addison-Wesley Publishing Company, 1985.

Dugan, M. T., J. A. Gentry, and K. A. Shriver. "The X-11 Model: A New Analytical Review Technique for the Auditor," *Auditing: A Journal of Practice & Theory* (Spring 1985): 11–22.

Foster, G. *Financial Statement Analysis.* Englewood Cliffs, New Jersey: Prentice-Hall, Inc., 1978.

Fox, J. *Linear Statistical Models and Related Methods.* New York: John Wiley & Sons, Inc., 1984.

Kenny, D. A. *Correlation and Causality.* New York: John Wiley & Sons, Inc., 1979.

Kinney, W. R., Jr., and G. L. Salamon. "Regression Analysis in Auditing: A Comparison of Alternative Investigation Rules," *The Journal of Accounting Research* (Autumn 1982): 350–366.

Peter, L. J. *Peter's Quotations—Ideas for Our Time.* New York: Bantam Books, 1977.

Sullivan, W. G., and W. W. Claycombe. *Fundamentals of Forecasting.* Reston, Virginia: Reston Publishing Company, 1977.

Willis, R. E. *A Guide to Forecasting for Planners and Managers.* Englewood Cliffs, New Jersey: Prentice-Hall, Inc., 1987.

Willis, R. E., and N. L. Chervany. *Statistical Analysis and Modeling for Management Decision-Making.* Belmont, California: Wadsworth Publishing Company, 1974.

Index

About the Author

THOMAS E. McKEE is Professor of Accountancy at East Tennessee State University, and is a CPA, CMA, CIA. His research has appeared in articles in *The Journal of Accountancy, The CPA Journal, The Journal of Accounting Education, Internal Auditor,* and *Management Accounting.*

Cold Stone, White Lily

Cold Stone, White Lily

Anne Markham Bailey

Copyright ©, 2011, Anne Markham Bailey

Published by

The Friends of Julian
St Julian's Alley
Rouen Road
Norwich
NR1 1QT
United Kingdom

www.friendsofjulian.org

Manufactured in the United States
First edition, first printing

ISBN 978-0-9541524-4-4

Title pages: Lily Scanograph by Neko Linda
Grimm, 2011.

Please visit www.coldstonewhitelily.com for more
information about this book.

These poems were written by Anne Wyngfield, a fourteenth-century English anchoress created by the poet Anne Markham Bailey. The setting is Bishop's Lynn, now King's Lynn, in East Anglia, United Kingdom.

Contents

Anne Wyngfield Timeline

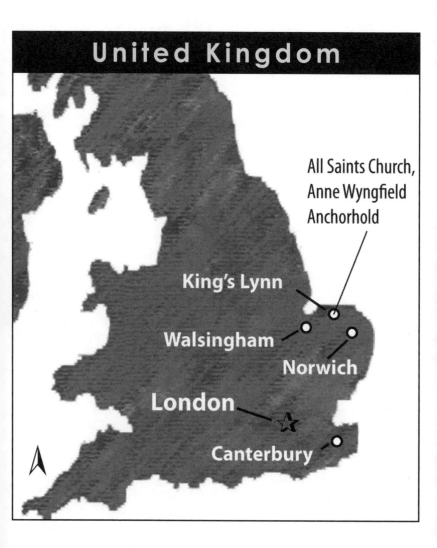

United Kingdom

All Saints Church,
Anne Wyngfield
Anchorhold

King's Lynn

Walsingham

Norwich

London

Canterbury

Poems

Apology

I am not a great poet like some of my compatriots. I lack imagination and skill. Still, I love words, the breath of communication, the vibrations of speech, the shapes of words on the page, the scratch of the quill on vellum. My hands are joyful when filled with a book. The thickness of a spine between thumb and finger, the scrape of turning pages are a fine song for a woman like me, who holds the shapes of words as friends.

When my lines are ill-composed and dull, think kindly of me and indulge me a little. I am not the champion of English verse, but I so want to speak to you, to sift the bits of all these years, to build small containers of memory to offer to you.

I am well-versed in human solitude, sharing time with my Lord. I am well-versed too in the suffering with which we dwell. Even the vessel of our salvation can rot and take on water, failing the faithful in the journey. I look in my heart and see the stain, but that is not all. There is love.

Because I am here, I set letters side-by-side, partner words in a dance. I toss gems in the air so that love will rain down.

–AW

Naissance

The stone aperture is a birth canal.
Clouds speed by as in a dream.
I am waking.
Cloud and sun,
billows of mist run round,
transparent.
We are born alone.
I am alone, sing to the mist,
test the stretch of breath,
listen for wings pitched in a minor key.
I well up from within,
chant communion, shimmer,
transgress in starched glints of doubt.
I am a white bird with hollow bones for flight.
I light on the pliant branch of bare faith, agog.
This closed door is an anchor.
I am free.

Flame

When I was a girl
I prayed before bed,
beheld the crucifix
on the opposite wall.
From dark sleep
I opened my eyes.
I lay on my side,
face to the wall,
back to my sister,
late in the night.
The wall breathed
beside me,
a sheet of flame
roaring
as flame roars.
I did not move,
my open body
waited for heat,
the dance of flame
on my heart,
as streaming stars
stare on winter nights
when folk sleep,
the Passion
constellated in fire.

May Day

The morning soared
with the river birds.
I was the first up
and dressed in the
dreaming house.
I shrugged the kirtle
over my shoulders,
snugged the hood
around my face.
I pulled the thick cloak
off the hook.
I strapped on the pattens
to keep my shoes clean
in the spring mud.
I walked to the clearing
where the pole stood tall.
Hopeful smoke
rose from
the center hole
of a little hut.
As I came close,
I heard murmurs and rustles

from inside and stopped,
but they heard my
movement in the field.
Molly and Joe emerged,
steaming bowls in their hands,
laughing in the air,
and asked me in.
As I entered,
I saw the flowers and the ribbons
for the baskets and our hair.
Molly pulled off my hood,
measured my head
in the petaled room.
Which will it be, Miss Anne?
I'll have it ready for you tonight.
I picked pink and white
to anchor a sheer veil,
adorned for the midnight dance.

Thirteen

I set the carding comb on the shelf,
stretched my arms alongside my ears,
raised my eyebrows at Mother,
who smiled and nodded her head.
I skipped to the house,
tied the leather bag around my waist,
patting the Psalter.
The scrip over my shoulder,
I loaded bread and hard cheese.
The green kirtle's tippets
swung long and loose
like my uncovered hair
sprinkled with lavender water.
My pointed leather shoes
were ready for the road,
running toward Lynn
to the barley fields
where I read psalms and sky,
my fingers ink-stained
from my practice as a scribe,
longing for a psalter of their own.
I prayed for Mother

after Father left for the Crusades.
She did not laugh
in the morning like before.
May Christ's fire wrap around her
and warm her with His passion.
She was too thin,
worked late into the night,
visited the tenants,
reckoned the figures.

First Kiss

The tall boy waited
in a bowing oak grove
in layered summer light,
nestled between thick roots,
a giant's thighs,
back against the grizzled bark,
chewing sweet grass,
twirling the stem.
I lied to mother,
said poor Emily was sick
and needed a visit.
William expected me.

He heard the twigs snap
and stood to face me.
He took my basket and
headed down the stony path
to the singing river.
We settled on a slate shelf
jutting above the shallow pool.
I took off my slippers and hose,
lifted my skirts,
and slipped my feet in the water,
the basket of wine and biscuits
covered in muslin in the warm sun.

He waded in and slipped on the rocks,
flapping his arms for balance.
He cocked his sun-bleached head,
held my green eyes with his brown ones,
and joggled his eyebrows.
I laughed and splashed my feet.

He tracked the small, silent fish,
glinting blue in the light.
He paused above the biggest
and thrust his hands into the pool.
He rose with a cry,
and there was the spotted fish,
flipping out of his hands
in streaming water,
falling back into the pool and away.
He whistled "Sumer is acomen,"
laughed, and fell quiet.

Anne, he said. *Your eyes are green
like the trees. Your dress is green
like the trees.*
He swooped in
and kissed my mouth
quick and light

like catching fish.
My toes
and my calves
and between my legs burned.
My cheeks flamed.
I did not look at him.

The sky darkened.
Drops soft as first kisses
fell in the still pool,
spread across the water
like the burning in a girl.
He pulled a cloth from his bag
and draped it over us
on the stone shelf,
I put my head on his shoulder
and fell asleep.

Are you awake, Anne?
I opened my eyes and closed them again.
The rain settled down.
No, I said.
What do you want me to look at? I asked.
The water is reflecting the sky.
He squeezed my hand.
I opened my eyes to the pool,
to a sky entirely new.

Betrothal

William rode in
to visit Father and Mother
on an early morning in June
before the ringing sky
clouded for the day.
High flying gulls
cried in arcs and fell away.
I watched him come,
fixed and pliant on the bay,
his long thighs relaxed.
He swung off,
handed the reigns to Philip,
the stuttering stable boy.
William hummed low,
like when my head
was on his chest,
listening at dusk
in our grassy dip
in the riverbank,
his arm around my shoulder.
He glanced up at the house,
his face pale.
He coaxed dust from his tunic,
arranged his leggings,

stamped his boots,
wiped his face with a small cloth
and combed his sandy hair with his fingers.
He paused for a drink
from the big wooden spoon,
approached the door
and stepped out of my sight.
I sat reading, vellum pages on the table,
waiting for Mother to call.

Ninth Month

Red flint winked on the road,
and I picked it up,
so full of child it was not easy
to bend and
fold toward the ground.
I tucked the stone
in the pouch at my waist.
The baby kicked, taking my breath.

Nine months before I gasped
on top my husband William.
I rubbed the tight skin with almond oil,
William cupped my belly,
nuzzled my neck and kissed the folds
of my breasts, my nipples dark, wide, round.
The baby moved inside me.
Ten months before
my breasts were small,
my belly flat and smooth.
The midwife said that grace grew
in the room inside me,
walls of flesh.

I held the soft swollen space,
the motion of William
behind me on the bed.
He held my hips,
set my bulging breasts to swinging.
Our baby shifted inside me.
I backed up to him
on my knees, and closed my eyes.
We rocked and breathed,
rode a pearl-crusted carriage.
Oh my Anne, oh my Anne,
he moved in and back,
cupping my belly as the baby swam.
I laughed and growled;
he groaned deep inside me.
Later, the three of us slept.

I went to church with Mother,
knelt before the altar,
grunting and short of breath.
She supported my elbow,
tucked a stray strand of hair,
stroked my cheek.
I looked to Mary, mother of salvation.

She fed us in our suffering
the warm milk of love.
I rubbed the small of my back
and laced my fingers under my belly.

The child big in me,
I waddled and smiled,
crossed the meadow,
eased down in the grass.
In the sun, my belly flexed;
the birth would be soon.

Plague

If you can, imagine
a sky raining daffodils
and daisies one morning,
and the next, the flowers
are dead rats and buboes;
yet the sun rises still
and moonlight casts shadows
as when William and I stretched
in the summer field
the year before.
After the fever's reign,
the moon lit up
bodies stacked in holes
like open mouths,
the earth hungry for
blisters and blood.
Souls fled from the stink,
the entire town
rank, a stiff fear,
each of us
fallen and torn,
an end without rites.

In the nicker of horses
and in the rutted creak of carts,
the wealthy fled early on,
some of the merchants too,
to remote places in the north
without pustules or public access.
We sent William and the children.
At Lynn, I pressed ginger to the sores
and brewed tinctures to heal,
but nothing stopped the skeleton,
the hiss in the cracks
of our homes and in our beds.
The tears of corpses
muddied the streets,
covered our shoes.
We stumbled pale
or sat in doorways,
whispering mercies,
screaming at God,
mumbling revenge,
as we cast bodies into the gullet
of the rapacious earth.

Death

When dying left my town of Lynn
to dance on other shreds of living,
singing did not build the morning fire
or humming fold the linen sheets
nor whistling tend the sheep,
as it was with my people.
The Anglian mist settled in at noon,
muted the purple loose strife's roar.
We heard the wind in the oak leaves.
The lapwing darted with the plover.

My family did not escape—
my Claire was gone.
My white-haired girl,
my peerless pearl,
asleep in my arms,
or high on William's shoulders,
settling clover crowns on her brothers.
Claire died far from Lynn,
far from the tattered girls
I held who moaned and ceased,
dumb with death.

I was a hollow mother;
I begged God to take us back,
to dance again in May,
laughing ribbons in our hair.

The wind blew across the river
where I walked each day;
William asked to walk with me.
I walked alone in meadowsweet,
mute in the howling silence
of emptied arms.
I went to the dank church.
We were a blasted, speechless folk,
we knelt on the carved slate slabs,
we bowed down before our Lord,
we asked forgiveness,
we lit candles for the dead,
we fell asleep on stone
and woke to pray
that we would sing again.

The Call

The boys rode away,
off to serve Edward of Woodstock,
to fight with France again.
They turned the horses in circles,
spurred them on,
raised dust, whooped and
laughed, glanced at me
choked with tears.
They swooped close to kiss me,
dark cloaks lifting like wings.
They planned for the falcons
during their absence,
brought gifts to the tenants.
Years before, I ran the house with my husband,
managed the rents and the weaving
when we slept wrapped liked sheets,
the babies between us,
Williams's arm steady on my chest.
I sleep alone now.
We are all called.
We listen across time.
These green meadows and sturdy villages,

the miracle plays, the poems sung in the valleys,
the devouring evil of two centuries past,
let us tell of it in English.
The boys reared their horses,
roared away.
The Virgin made Mother,
breasts round with grace, offers us drink.
As the Lord was born of Mary,
a true body, like mine,
the word made flesh,
the blood of His mercy
called me, asked me to serve.

Censing Angels

Why did I marry spirit,
promise my years to stones
where fungi and spiders stretch?

The chalice is filled.
The host is lifted and offered.
Censing angels beat wings;
veils of smoke cross the altar.

The Holy Ghost surrounds the Father.
Mother Mary sits quiet,
her plump son on her lap.

I kneel at the unseen window
of the suspirating cell,
a jawbone in a silver box
on my altar of shifting light.

My people suffer so.
The priest chants
bungled Latin.
Censing angels swirl
in the air; their incense pots sparkle.
My faith is re-born
in wings of smoke and stone.

White Lily

From the mounded snow
she pushes green-bodied,
hungry for spring sky.
She reaches thin-veined arms,
trailing draping fingers
in the blood of Christ,
and mourns a mother's loss.
She rides the sunny arc of day,
dreams the lift and drop
of moon-bleached stone
touching the boundary of her bed.
Her buds swell.

Blood

A mix of nettles, the ash of roses,
and a little red wine calmed
the vigorous flow of blood
flagrant in the anchor hold.
From prayers on high
to the flood down low,
woman is not evil
or soiled
or born of sin.
Blood is the sacrifice.
The world is reborn
year after year,
slippery skinned babies
suckling like drunks
as I suckle at the breast of Christ.

Cold

In the arms of my Lord
I wake, sing prayers
in the dark,
burn in love
on a night so cold,
an embrace of snow
round singing stone.

Pilgrims

I heard the jangling and calling,
the stamping and wrangling,
long before I saw the pilgrims,
passing the fields I roamed as a girl,
grassy scents like gold to me.
On their way to Walsingham
to the Shrine of the Blessed Virgin,
they stopped at Lynn to rest and eat
and care for the sick.
They camped in the churchyard
outside my hold and came to the window.
Anchoress Anne, Anchoress Anne!
A murmur began
in the line of folk,
various and sundry,
gems strung together
to be cleansed in Mary's grace.
I looked at the
plucked foreheads,
and the bent tonsures.
I heard a visionary howl.
A barefoot man stooped,
pocked with sin.

A baby slept slung
to the chest of a young mother.
Please pray for us, they asked,
and I did. I do.
When the pilgrims settled down
in the yard around the church,
the brothers of Black Friars
bustled around them, unspeaking.
I closed the black cloth,
bowed down before my Lord,
tears of his blood in my heart.
May my people be lifted,
like pearls tossed high
or diamonds in gold crowns.
The sweet grass under my body
is an open field.
I laugh with outstretched arms
as Father scoops me up,
puts me on his shoulder,
takes me home.

Matins

In a small walled garden,
peony and ginger,
gromwell and gillyflower
burst under the sun,
inviting me to scent and shine.

I am on my knees on a cold floor.

I enter the arbor like a warm kitchen
or two bodies fitted together.
Mother Mary stands —
the blue cloth of her gown
dark in the folds,
her face framed in white,
her eyes soft, holding me,
her hands open as questions.

I am on my knees on a cold floor.

Around the wall,
wild geranium, meadow cress,
and morning glory sing to Mary.

Lifting their bloom
and sharpening their color,
they press their fragrance
that she should be pleased.
The mound of roses
curls and sparkles
as Mother brings me home.

Wool Gown

This wool gown
is like sheep in fields
of morning sun.
They shake their ears,
drop their heads,
pull soft grass,
silver and wet,
from the sleeping ground.

Where I climbed,
the hawks cried
above the high, twisted oak.
My pocket full of book,
I lay along the thick branch,
reached for the psalter,
the smooth cover supple
with eager turning.
The leaves fell open.

Mary is afraid.
Gabriel whispers in her ear.
Her face is pale but shines

from the news.
Logos is living in the oak.

I leave the window and the mass,
full of the Host.
I am a guest in this space.
Wool kisses my thin ankles
sheathed in linen.

Leaving the Window

The lilies bowed
at the feet of the
fretting mother.
Golden stamens,
long, thick stalks bended to her.
She wrapped around
her fevered bundle,
his eyes too bright.
The lilies nuzzled her dress
as she patted and sang;
her elbow cradled his head,
his cheeks too red.
His mother willed
him to be well,
to run about her skirts,
playing with sticks for the fire.
She offered the child.
I lifted him into the hold.
Her sore eyes
counted fruitless harvests,
reckoned leveling cold,
her husband's sharp slaps

and dry mountings.
You'll tend him, she said.
She pulled the hood
around her face, turning back.
I nodded with the lilies,
left the window with the boy,
and rocked in the damp scent
of bodies in linen and wool,
sweetgrass underfoot.
I brewed St. John's Wort
plucked wild on Midsummer's Eve,
mixed in honey,
and let it cool.
As he drank,
I knelt silent in
the union of gnosis,
dropped lonely pearls on stone,
holding the sleeping boy.
I prayed for mother and son,
Blessed Virgin, heal us.
I held the throated tune of the lily,
the fragrant surety of open heart.

Flint

Crosses line the church
in grey and yellow and red,
flint knapped in circles
of men who share stories
as they work, slapping the stone
with their hammers.
The yard around the church
crunches thick from years
of building and repair.
On my way to the anchor hold
after the Last Rites,
I picked up a piece
and put it in my pocket.
It is now on my altar,
the outside rough,
the inside secret,
smooth and milky,
a frozen sea.

Winter

In February, the sun is weak.
Snow gloves the hold.
I wear all my clothes day and night,
my cloak as well,
and drink hot broth.
At the grey altar I call my Lord.

Heat this freezing woman, Lord,
with the heated arms of your passion.
Heat my soul with faith
so hot that cold and wind don't sting.

Forehead on my clasped, numb hands,
legs needled from kneeling,
shivers running up and down
the length of me,
tears in my eyes,
heart punctured and open.

Father, your son hung naked on the cross
for love of me and had no regrets.
Father, teach me such love
to heat and succor this cold, weeping world.

I called to my Father,
His Son before me
on the blood-soaked ground,
head hung upon his chest,
spikes driven through hands and feet,
flesh ragged and torn beneath his weight
upon the cross, all alone, for me.
A wall of fire rose up behind him,
and in my belly and in my cheeks
the fire lifted, roared behind
my suffering Christ,
naked, hung for love,
no snow or cold to damp the flame,
as when I was a girl,
held in the burning arms of God.

Blazing

Stone darkens
after blazing;
I lie the length of flame,
the length of my frame,
not seeking the cool
white of the lily but blazing,
limpid on the slate floor.
I touch the walls;
my cheeks burn.
The blessed belly of my heat
calls for release,
calls for my Savior.

English Bible

A grey hood of fog
protected the anchor hold.
I knelt at the altar,
my eyes on the crucifix,
the pain and rapture of
the Lord in my heart,
tears pouring as blood
poured from his wounds.
How long I was there,
one with my Lord,
I don't know,
a stillness like pearls
in the hold,
turtle doves in the oaks,
the turtu repeated, the shuffle of wings.
A voice sounded at the squint,
—Anchoress Anne, it's Thomas.
Please come to the window.
I pulled the black cloth back,
glanced past him.
He opened a vellum wrapper
with nervous hands,

his index finger ink-stained.
I nodded my head,
reached for the Bible,
smiled at Thomas.
—Are you sure, Anne?
It might mean death by fire.
I met his red-rimmed eyes,
brought the book to my chest.
Logos illumined was our work
and our earthly trial.
I strapped the book beneath the altar.
—Go, Thomas. Go. Now we must
teach the people to read.

Morning

The light is white morning.
I turn from belly to side,
cradle shoulder and hip.
The damp exhale of linen
under wool is the mist
outside thick stone and me.
My Lord is my mother
licking crusted eyelids.

Audience with the Bishop

I was told he would arrive within the week.
On the seventh day of afternoon rain
with rumors of burnings at Norwich,
the open spaces choked in stink,
black cheering and tongue wagging,
Burn the heretic! The fiend will burn!
flame melted flesh into smoke and ash,
and Sawtre was dragged from Lynn
by the hard holy men.
The splashing of horses in the yard,
the sharp, shrill voices,
and hurried cluster of footsteps
announced that he was come for me.

My sisters served hot brew and cold biscuits,
and I asked His Eminence to pray with me
to soften his hard questions,
(Do you favor the English Bible?)
to knead the rigid space between us,
(Do you give communion?)
to murmur the teaching of our Savior,

(Are you loyal to seclusion?)
to kneel at the altar, side by side.

In the heat of my thin hands,
the gift of Christ's anguish
shimmered like the gold threads
in the Bishop's robes.
The Bishop lifted thick grey fingers,
plucked up a biscuit,
and turned it round to study,
sharp eyes squinting in the dim light.
He lowered his hand,
tapping the simple fare against the plate
and stretching the corners of his unsmiling mouth,
sniffed the treasure of a plain, wool gown,
draped the weight of a ruby thumb.

Bel-Dame

Edward called at the window today,
Clara Wyngfield new-born in his arms,
a plump daughter, green-eyed like Edward and me.
Her reach ends with fingers,
lips flexed in an O,
ready for a breast
bulging with milk.
Edward offers her to me.
I cup her head in lonely hands,
her back along my forearms.
If I put her to my chest,
she will root for the breast and cry,
feeling tricked.

I am the bel-dame.
Across harvests and slaughters
my well-sucked teats
hang lean and slack under my chemise.
I hold Clara eye to eye,
nuzzling her close,
kiss her nose to nose,
graze cheek on cheek,

and hum the old tune of swollen breasts
as under apple blossoms
on the cloth that William spread,
I reached for Edward to ease
the swell of milk in me
and the baby kneaded the mound,
prompting the flow,
milk spray like stamens
shooting down his throat.
As I hold Clara,
smelling her close,
my breasts vibrate,
my womb contracts,
and my cunt hums,
blessing the girl.

Last Poem

When the lily frees her petals
onto the dark earth of my seventieth year,
I sit and smile at her vigor.
Bloom runs in her, pushes her
to unfold golden throats to the sky,
to stretch open-blanched petals flecked with pink,
like fleet fish on running days of warm stone.
I sit in the garden, still but for breathing,
head and feet bare, a thin old woman in the sun.
The May wind scatters apple blossoms,
white boats riding the air,
a chaotic phalanx
of single-winged angels,
children loosed from a captive home
after days of gasping cold.
I drift in the thrum of bees,
the smallest of birds
indolent with industry,
proboscis intent on honey and wax.

My back to the hold,
I relax in the old chair
whose grain I feel like my skin.
A pair of turtle doves
purrs on the roof, backdrop for wind and bees.
They mate a single time for all the days and nights
or remain in lonely faith, not choosing again.
She plucks under-feathers, thick and soft,
lines the nest for her eggs, for her fledglings
while her mate pushes air through his throat,
accompanies the bees, ruffles in the petaled wind.

At my waist I wear a small red bag,
my father's gift sixty years ago.
I open the bag,
draw out the flint
with my talons sharp,
like William's falcons
flexed around the gauntlet.
But mine are stiffly hooked
and do not straighten now.
In my palm I lift the stone relic,
not saints' remains but holy,

spied on the road
when my body grew big,
my belly like the hold,
my babies enclosed as I am.
I listened for their voices.
I pushed them to my arms.
We are all pilgrims,
in wombs and anchor holds,
the gardens in spring,
love at the core.

They took Sawtre two years ago
from Lynn and locked him up.
I slipped him an embroidered cloth
to feed his courage,
a threaded lion sleeping with one
open eye; like Jesus crucified,
the flesh dies but spirit lives.
Sawtre burned in March.
After nineteen days of torture
in a cell not built for human life,
like mine is, where I control the door,
he took back his word.

Burn me instead, I sang.
If I were in that square,
roped upon the pole,
flame leaping at my feet
like foaming dogs in a pack,
I would be curled
deep in the night,
in a cold, stone cell,
in a barley field in summer
or astride my muscled husband.
My Lord's call is flame.
I am old and dry.
I ignite in a rush,
kiss my Lord,
and fly.

The Historical Context

Anne Wyngfield's life mirrored the century in which she lived. Fourteenth-century England was a time of lush creative and spiritual expression as well as of enormous suffering. Poets such as Geoffrey Chaucer, William Langland, and the *Gawain*-poet wrote foundational works of literature in English. Christian mystical experience flourished and prompted the development of a well-textured vocabulary of devotion in the vernacular. Because the predominant context of the society was religious, both space and objects within that space were rife with sacred symbolism. The Catholic Church was the frame for the sacred life, but the frame was cracking. Both Church and monarchy fought long and costly wars over spiritual and geographic territories. In 1315, England suffered a devastating famine due to extreme weather conditions and intense cold. In 1349, the Plague decimated almost half of the population. This loss in population led to long-term social shifts, which the reigning powers attempted to control or eradicate. For the first time people sensed that they might gain more control of their lives outside the feudal and Church hierarchy, for example by being literate and exploring a direct relationship with God in the vernacular.

Such was the historical setting of Anne Wyngfield, who lived in Bishop's Lynn, Norfolk, in the region of East Anglia. Bishop's Lynn was a busy port town on the Ouse River north of Cambridge and the Fens. Major east-west and north-south roads join at Lynn. Just north, the sea pushes into a bowl-like shape of land called The Wash at the mouth of the Ouse River. Norwich is about fifty miles from Lynn. Lynn housed four communities of mendicants—the Carmelites, Franciscans, Dominicans, and Augustinians.

Anne shared the century with the writers who gave birth to a body of early English literature. For the first time, English was used as a written language to describe complex feelings and thoughts. Speakers of English became writers of English and readers, or would-be readers, which had enormous social implications. Poets Chaucer and Langland described their societies in the vernacular. Their works were some of the first social commentary in English on English society. Mystics, such as Julian of Norwich, Richard Rolle, Walter Hilton, and the anonymous author of the *Cloud of Unknowing* also made important written contributions in English. In general, they put forth that the highest human act is union with God. Delivered in English, this message of a direct relationship with God influenced the population.

Within the Church, however, Latin remained the language of God, and God was accessed through the Church. Not everyone agreed with the Church, however. John Wycliffe, a great scholar at Oxford, translated the Bible into English. He and the Lollards, who followed his teaching, insisted that each person has a right to a personal relationship with God and should be able to access the Holy Word of God in the vernacular. Thus, Wycliffe paved the way for the English Reformation. The Church's reaction to the Wycliffe and Lollard assertion was predictable. The

Church strongly opposed the diminishment of its power as the broker of religion.

Some individual priests supported translating the Bible and the Wycliffe view. William Sawtre, Rector of St. Margaret's Church at Lynn, advocated the use of an English Bible. As a result, he was arrested and taken from Lynn. He was tortured for nineteen days in the "Cell of Little-Ease." At the end of nineteen days, he recanted his position but was burned nonetheless. Sawtre was the first to be charged and burned, but many fell under the suspicion of Bishop Henry Despenser, who ruled from Norwich Cathedral with a sinister fist.

Despite the Church's intention to maintain control, the fourteenth century saw a tremendous rise in Christian mystics and visionaries. Aside from the classic canon of English mystics, a plethora of visionaries claimed to have seen Jesus and the Virgin Mary in a variety of visitations. These visions were often passionate portrayals of scenes from the life of Christ with vivid descriptions of flowing blood and tears. The corporeal experience of union was a prime visionary focus expressed in the language of lovers. The visionaries were often required to defend themselves from charges of heresy and to prove that the vision was divine rather than demonic.

In 1349, the Black Plague struck England. The first wave that blew in from Asia via Europe was ferocious, cutting the population almost in half. Those who had second homes in remote areas fled the towns and cities. The population did not know the cause of the pestilence. People thought that the Plague was God's punishment for their sins, or a plot by the Jews, who were said to have poisoned the wells, or perhaps the work of foreigners or lepers.

Great social and economic change occurred as a result of the Plague. These changes set the scene for the Peasants' Revolt of 1381, the first stirring of a social reform movement in England. At this time, England shifted from a sedentary to a mobile society. With so many dead from the Plague, labor was scarce. The historical structure of manorial control over the lives of the workers changed. Serfs and villeins, who had been tied to manor estates, commanded higher wages and many left their ancestral lands. In Lynn, a large number of laborers took over farms and estates abandoned due to the Plague. The monarchy tried to impose wage caps and to slow the tide of change by instituting the Sumptuary Laws, designed to regulate and reinforce traditional social hierarchy by restricting clothing, food, labor, and travel, but these were ineffective. In some cases, the landowners themselves raised the labor prices as they bid against one another.

Travel gained enormous appeal, and pilgrimage to holy shrines increased in popularity. On pilgrimage, people of different social strata came into contact in a new way for the first time on the field of devotion. Some of the major sites were Canterbury, which housed the relics of St. Thomas Beckett, and Walsingham, a site devoted to the Virgin Mary. Lynn was a stopping place and staging site for pilgrims traveling to Walsingham, arguably the most holy shrine of the Blessed Virgin in the fourteenth century. Pilgrims stopped at Lynn to rest and prepare for the final stages of the pilgrimage, most of which they walked barefoot. The monarchy tried to stop the flow of people around the country but had little effect.

The phenomena of pilgrimage showed that English society was cohesively Christian with few exceptions. Edward I expelled the Jews from England in 1290. Religion and the possibility of salvation were the over-riding concerns of the entire society. The spiritual and political power of the Church was eroding. Flagrant abuses of wealth and power inflamed the population while the divisiveness of the Western Schism raised doubt concerning the divine authority of the Pope. In addition, a growing number of people claimed a direct relationship with God outside the Church. Even so, the ordering of society was based on religion—particularly its relation to time. The world was ordered according to Church time.

Anne Wyngfield experienced the restricted choices of fourteenth-century women. She ultimately decided to make her own choice from the few available, and she became an anchoress at All Saint's Church at Lynn. In so doing she joined a long anchoritic lineage stretching back to the Desert Fathers. She stepped out of quotidian life and into a life rich with religious symbolism. From the plants in the garden outside the anchor hold, to the saint's relic upon her altar, to the mass that she could witness in the church from a small window in her cell, everything was steeped with meaning, containing a story to be read. The enclosed garden outside the anchor hold was a tribute to the Virgin Mary with symbolic flowers like the rose without thorns while the violet stood for the Virgin as a humble being without sin.

A community of readers spread across Europe, sharing manuscripts and ideas through a network of traveling religious persons. Both men and women participated in this movable library, and, thus, ideas spread across Europe. This interchange indicates that an anchoress was not buried alive in any sense of the word but was part of a vibrant international community.

The anchoress is commonly portrayed as a woman buried alive, proclaimed dead to the world, never to emerge again. The picture that I saw in August 2008 from visits to four anchor hold sites in England was quite different. Many anchor holds have been used as vestries for hundreds of years, but inspection of the architectural remnants makes it apparent that the holds were actually small apartments that allowed access to the inside of the church, to a small garden, to the servants, and to the public. The reality supports the *The Ancrene Riwle's* description of an apartment with a room for the anchoress, a parlor of sorts for receiving visitors, and a room for two servants. The apartment (also cell or hold) contained several windows, one between the anchoress and her servants and one facing into the church, usually close to the altar, and one to the outside. No doubt she lived an austere life with few physical comforts and with the strenuous practices of her office.

Although part of the Enclosure Ceremony did include the Last Rites, the anchoress was not "dead to the world" in the common sense. The ceremony honored the significant shift in her status. She was no longer a simple part of quotidian life but had chosen to live apart and to serve God and community as her life's work. As Christ had been re-born, so had she.

The Life of Anne Wyngfield

The poems in this work, *Cold Stone, White Lily,* take place in medieval England. The poems are written from the point of view of a fourteenth-century English anchoress, an urban Christian woman recluse. Her name is Anne Wyngfield, and she is from an area in East Anglia called Bishop's Lynn, later changed to King's Lynn during the Reformation. In the poems, Anne looks back across her life from her position as an elderly anchoress.

As a member of the county gentry, Anne's father Robert owned and managed an estate outside of Lynn. Anne's mother Clara came from a prosperous merchant family. Although their marriage was a successful business arrangement, a true romance existed between the two. Her parents Robert and Clara Sampson had four children of whom only Anne and her brother Edward survived into adulthood. Robert and Clara leased land to tenants in a shifting economic landscape due in part to a labor shortage following the plague. They also raised livestock. Although they were a well-to-do family, their home consisted of a large wooden hall with stables attached.

The Sampson family's high level of literacy was uncommon in the fourteenth century, especially among women. Clara Sampson, however, was from the merchant class, giving her more mobility and access to teachers and manuscripts than was available to most women. She wanted to learn. Before moving to Lynn to marry Robert, she read English, French, and Latin. Robert was not so educated, but he was capable and practical. Anne and Edward learned to read from Clara. Texts were scarce at this time, but the monastics in Lynn participated in an unofficial lending community as manuscripts spread across England and the Continent. The Sampsons were generous supporters of the monasteries, and they were included in the community of readers. Clara proved a capable business woman, a devout Christian, and a keen wit. She lived in a society in which noble women were severely restricted, but, despite her move into the gentry, she insisted upon the freedoms allowed the merchant class. When her husband went off to the Hundred Years' War, she ably oversaw the running of the estate. She and Robert raised their children to work hard and to ponder deeply.

A bright and curious girl, Anne lived with great vivacity and spiritual longing. She tended toward the visionary as evidenced by the dreams that she shared with her parents. She was a person who wanted to help others, drawn to the suffering people of the world. As an adolescent, she asked her parents to allow her to become an anchoress, but her parents refused because the life of an anchoress was so austere. Her parents did not want to lose their singing daughter. Anne acquiesced.

Later, as a teenager, she married William Wyngfield, also from Lynn, with whom she was deeply in love. Her brother Edward was killed as a young man when a horse fell on him. William and Anne inherited the Sampson estate and had three children—Clara, Edward, and William Walter. Clara died in the Plague far from Lynn where Anne remained to help care for the poor. Anne was devastated by the loss of her daughter. Slowly, William and Anne rebuilt their lives and their hearts.

In 1355, William went off to serve Edward of Woodstock in the Battle of Poitiers. He was killed in 1368. Anne and the boys continued on amid the turmoil of a changing society. In 1369, the boys left to serve the king, and Anne then felt the call that she'd heard as a girl. She petitioned the Bishop of Norfolk Henry Despenser to become an anchoress at All Saints Church in Lynn. She was able to show financial independence and piety and was accepted. Thus, in 1370, she was formally enclosed as an anchoress. Anne chose a life of prayer, contemplation, and community service. For a woman in the fourteenth century with few lifestyle choices, she made a radical claim of freedom in order to pursue an ultimate union with the Divine—not just for herself, but for her whole community.

Anne was a devout practitioner. Her life as an urban recluse was not a dry and lifeless affair but a passionate journey. In the fourteenth century, women's devotional imagery was replete with splendid and detailed images of the sufferings of Christ, highlighting the flow of tears and blood in particular. The descriptive devotional language often portrayed Christ as lover and knight with much sexual innuendo in some cases. Anne lived a disciplined and ordered life of practice, following the Liturgical Hours and the Church Calendar. She served the community as an advocate and counselor, particularly as the punitive Poll Taxes created suffering and unrest among the already struggling poor.

Anne had been trained as a scribe when she was a girl. She enjoyed this work tremendously. She wrote and participated in the community of the literate, deciding to write this series of poems in later life. She supported the creation of an English Bible, a radical political position, especially for a person of the Church. She wanted to teach people to read so that they could form their own relationships with God rather than relying on the Church whose unbounded greed and divisiveness cast a shadow on its role as divine intermediary. Anne wished for others to experience the intensely personal relationship with God that fueled her life. Being able to read God's Word in English would help

her people, she felt. Although it was danger-
ous and potentially heretical, she protected
one of the many manuscripts of the Wycliffe
Bible in her anchor hold.

Anne was not accused of heresy, yet she
was questioned by powerful Church leaders,
such as Bishop Despenser of Norwich. Over
the years, Anne developed as an authentic
leader with natural authority, much of which
was based on her personal relationship with
God. She understood that God is Love. Thus,
it was her responsibility to practice love on
earth. This practice did not sit well with
those whose practice was power and personal aggrandizement. Bishop Dispenser visited
Anne when he was in Bishop's Lynn. Many,
such as her good friend William Sawtre
Rector at St Margaret's Church, not far from
her anchor hold, were accused of heresy for
their support of the English Bible. Sawtre
was taken away from Lynn, tortured, and
tried. The Cell of Little-Ease was his torture
chamber. It did not permit him to sit, stand,
or lie down. After nineteen days, he recanted
his claim to a belief in a direct relationship
with Christ, free of Mother Church. He was

burned at the stake nonetheless in 1401, just before Anne died.

Anne Wyngfield died of old age in 1401. She was seventy-four years old, quite ancient by fourteenth-century standards. Anne embodied the passion that she understood and felt in the physical, emotional, intellectual, and spiritual realms of human and holy existence. She saw and held the world as sacred space, emanating from and containing her relationship with God. She believed that her life was about service—serving the world as Christ had through sacrifice and commitment.

Afterword

As an adolescent girl, I lay in my bed, thinking about my purpose in life. Two paths seemed plausible. I considered being a nun or being a soldier. As a nun I could spend my hours seeking union with God and doing good works. As a soldier I could provide protection from evil forces in the world. I remember weighing the two options to see which might be the best fit.

In my early years, I attended Brooke Hill School for Girls, a school atop Red Mountain in Birmingham, Alabama, where I grew up. The school was a kind of container in which girls shared space with other girls, and our value and experience was respected and shared, not trivialized. At Brooke Hill, we engaged fully in academics, sports, and extracurricular activities, developing into well-educated, independent-minded young women. In sixth grade, my teacher Blanche Black and my mother, who was our librarian and journalism teacher, developed the idea of making a movie about King Arthur, for our class was studying his legends. I was

Galahad. I found the Holy Grail in the woods behind the school in the Outdoor Classroom. It was a sailing trophy from our home covered with satin. My tunic was a dyed sheet and my helmet was corrugated board covered in tin foil. As I fell to my knees before the Grail, I hit a sharp, little rock, which caused rapture to flicker across my face as I prayed. Since then, I laugh and say that when you find the Holy Grail in sixth grade, what is there left to do in life? As an adult, I understand the Grail quest as a longing for the unitive experience of spirit made flesh, for a container in which that metamorphosis can take place.

Around the time of my confirmation in the Episcopal Church, when I was twelve years old, a priest commented lightly that I might be overly intense about Jesus. I don't remember his comment exactly, but I will never forget how I felt learning that my deep feeling of union with the Divine did not resonate with that priest or in that parish. After confirmation, I did not return to the church for years.

I attended Barnard College, the women's college at Columbia University. Barnard proved to be a supportive environment. When I graduated, I could not say what women had been doing throughout the periods of human history that I had been studying so avidly. For the most part, it seemed to me, we were a voiceless sex with little record of the past. Written records of our thoughts, dreams, and pursuits were sparse to non-existent, and our voices were largely unheard. Was I to conclude that we women were limited to doing laundry, birthing children, and running households? Were we limited to our corporeal world with no way to express the longings of our journey? What happened to women like me who thrived on intellectual and spiritual engagement and expression, who loved language and its artful use, who wrote and recorded their thoughts, feelings, and daily activities as I did? Looking to the past as a mirror for my future, I found an emptiness and a silence. Only later would I learn to look with different eyes and to listen for silence tuned to a frequency not silent at all.

After graduation from Barnard, I did not pursue a linear career path. What interested me most was the process in which my internal life meshed with the outside world. What career was that? I had majored in East Asian Studies (Chinese), but I was not interested in continuing in that field. I was a poet. I went to work to earn enough money to get by while I wrote and read, performed and sang. All things are fodder for this work.

I took a part-time job as a librarian at the smallest branch of the Birmingham Public Library in Wylam, Alabama, and a part-time job at my father's printing company. I travelled to China to explore career possibilities in publishing, and, serendipitously, learned about and entered an MFA program in Book Arts at the University of Alabama. As I was learning to print letterpress, set type by hand, make paper, and pare leather for book bindings, I worked, earned enough money to survive, and married a Columbia grad who had followed me home to Alabama. Our life was full of the sounds and textures of art, music, and late nights on an Alabama front porch.

Then I became pregnant and life changed. I became a mother and ancient instincts surfaced. My priorities shifted radically. Eventually the marriage unraveled. My young son was the primary foothold of my path at this time. I longed for a way to communicate from the depth of my being, and a phrase looped in my head, "I am here to let my light shine, and, if I cannot do that, then I don't want to do this."

Being the mother of Edward was rich and deeply fulfilling. His presence allowed me to pour love and nurturance onto him and, thus, into both of us. Our home was the safe and protective container that I sought for myself. And so we both developed along our own paths.

I was learning to be my own mother and to take care of and nurture my self. I recorded this process in poetry, prose, and drawings that became the dramatic monologue "I Dream a Mama." I performed the work at the Birmingham Museum of Art. As Edward grew, so did I. I expanded my business career in sales at the family company, started to read my poetry publicly, and saw some of my work published. I received grants to further my writing. I made paper and metal sculptures. Our life bubbled with creativity. We adopted the old man across the street who was alone in life. When he died, I wrote an essay about him called "Not Too Bad."

About this time a dear friend led me to mindfulness meditation, and, for the next ten years, I immersed myself in Shambhala Buddhism. Meditation is a slow process of profound discovery, an unpeeling of layers, an opening to the rawness and hurt not just in myself but in all humans. I committed to walk the path of the Bodhisattva, undertaking the practice of loving all beings as a life goal. I spent months in meditation retreat off and on over the years. I swam deep, unraveling the confusion. I journeyed to the core, and I was the core. Somewhere along the path, I yearned for my own culture, not feeling a deep kinship with the Tibetan symbols that mark Shambhala Buddhism. It was like being on a fantastic trip, aware of enormous transformation and growth, and one day you wake up and the season has changed, and it is time to go home. I discovered that the outward and inward life paths are not separate. They are one and the same.

The money-work, the creative-work, and the mother-work are not different paths.

When my son entered high school, I decided to pursue an old dream of studying creative writing and English literature, so I entered the MA in English Program at the University of Alabama in Birmingham. When I interviewed with the director, I told him that my poems were a secret I wanted to bring into the light. I soon met a wonderful professor Dr. Flowers Braswell, a medievalist, and took her course in Arthurian Legend, and went on to take as many of her classes as possible. I clearly remember the day when she said the word "anchoress."

At the same time I also enrolled in poetry workshops. The process of analyzing and critiquing my work in a group was just what I needed. I learned to take criticism so that I did not fear moving my work into the public domain as I had before. I became comfortable with myself as a poet at the age of 45. I set aside the critical voice that said that if I wasn't going to be the best poet on earth, then there was no value to my work at all. I discovered that the poet's path is to process experience and communicate effectively.

When the time came to shape the MA thesis, it occurred to me that I might speak in the voice of an anchoress and write a suite of poems from that point of view. As I considered this possibility, I realized that such a work would require detailed research so that the historical aspect was accurate. Not only would the historical overview be crucial, but so would every single detail in the poems. If my anchoress were to be plausible, her voice would have to be as authentic as possible. How could I achieve this when virtually no first-person records exist. Even the well-known work of Julian of Norwich had been recorded by a scribe.

The idea glittered in my heart and mind. I could reach out and give voice to a woman in medieval England who made a radical decision to leave her normal life based on the same thirst for the journey of spiritual union that I had experienced. Furthermore, I could study my own religious heritage from the point of view of a mystic in that tradition hundreds of years before my time. I could dig into the fabric of a woman's life — a woman who is a daughter, student, wife, mother, lover, thinker, and spiritual practitioner — a woman like me. Perhaps this project would be a way to write my own mythology and to fill in not just the gaps, but the gaping holes in the story of women.

I had come to understand through the arduous practice of meditation that our human desire for union in the ultimate sense, which all religions offer as the fruition of the journey, is actually the journey itself. Each moment along the way is the path. Divine union is what we are. The journey is the practice of developing the space, the eyes and ears of heart and mind that allow such truth to simply exist. The practice of settling the mind produces an uncluttered space that is necessary for love's blossoming. So too is there a need to be held or contained in a safe, quiet place like an anchoress's cell or in a meditation hall so that longing and fruition can unite in a metamorphosis.

Anne Wyngfield, my fourteenth-century English anchoress, transformed me in much the same way as my son Edward. In shaping her voice, I shaped my own. She and I share a journey of longing and action, of words gestated in silence. Our stories weave together as a bright light that is nurtured and welcomed through the crafting of an internal home, an anchor hold or Grail, where the sacred is gathered and held, to be shared by all.

The Friends of
Julian of Norwich

The Friends of Julian is an international body drawn from many different nations. Details of how to become a Friend are to be found on our website www.friendsofjulian. org.uk together with information about the core grouping, the Companions of Julian of Norwich, for those who wish to make a serious commitment to a Julian-inspired contemplative life in the secular world.

The Friends of Julian run the Julian Centre next door to the Julian Shrine in Norwich, England. The Centre houses a shop where books may be purchased together with other items of interest including a range of cards.

In addition to this present volume, The Friends has published other titles including those listed below, all of which are obtainable from the Centre.

FLOWERDEW, Jean. (2010) *The Anchoress: A Novel Set in Julian's Time for Older Children and Teenagers.*

FRUEWIRTH, Fr G. (2009) *Julian of Norwich and the Awakening of the Soul in the 21st Century.*

MCLEAN, M. (1984) *Who Was Julian? A Beginner's Guide.*

UPJOHN, S. (1979, 1992) *Mind Out of Time: A Play on Julian of Norwich and Her Significance.*

UPJOHN, S. (1992) *Julian of Norwich; All Shall Be Well: Daily Readings.*

Texts of the annual Julian lectures are also available and cover most of the lectures given in the past twenty-five years.

For more information: www.friendsofjulian.org.uk.